More Praise for
How Did I Not See This Coming?

"What lessons does a new manager need to learn to lead her team effectively? Katy Tynan shares the story of a young leader gaining insights through her own experiences and those of her colleagues."

—Jerry Davis
Professor of Management, Michigan Ross School of Business

"Katy Tynan's *How Did I Not See This Coming?* fulfills the promise of providing a useful—and entertaining—management book that tells the story about what managers need to learn and do to be great."

—David Grebow
CEO, KnowledgeStar

"Through an engaging story about a fictional employee who learns to be an effective manager, Katy Tynan lifts the veil on insecurities and self-doubt that every new manager feels, and then gives us the perspective and tools that help managers be successful. In the vein of *One Minute Manager,* the book uses storytelling to convey management concepts in an entertaining way that is a must-read for all new (and experienced) managers."

—Stephen Gill
Co-Founder, Learning to Be Great

"Written in the format of a novel, *How Did I Not See This Coming?* carries us from very bad days in the life of a manager to thankfully brighter and lighter days when the protagonist of the book can finally experience a career that makes sense. This book can carry YOU there too!"

—Ken Lizotte
Chief Imaginative Officer, emerson consulting group

"If you want to become a better manager, then you should read this book!"

—Jacob Morgan

Bestselling Author, Speaker, and Futurist

"A refreshing and engaging take on the transition to management that's both interesting to read and full of useful concepts for new leaders."

—Jeff Wald

Founder, WorkMarket

"In contrast to the countless jargon filled management guides, Katy Tynan provides clear, practical, and sage advice for any new or soon to be manager and those who help to develop them. The storytelling format is refreshingly entertaining and very effective."

—Daniel Lovely

Chief Learning Officer, AIG

HOW DID

WITHDRAWN

A NEW MANAGER'S

I NOT

GUIDE TO

AVOIDING

SEE THIS

TOTAL DISASTER

KATY TYNAN

COMING?

PRESS

© 2018 ASTD DBA the Association for Talent Development (ATD)
All rights reserved. Printed in the United States of America.

21 20 19 18   1 2 3 4 5

No part of this publication may be reproduced, distributed, or transmitted in any form or by any means, including photocopying, recording, or other electronic or mechanical methods, without the prior written permission of the publisher, except in the case of brief quotations embodied in critical reviews and certain other noncommercial uses permitted by copyright law. For permission requests, please go to www.copyright.com, or contact Copyright Clearance Center (CCC), 222 Rosewood Drive, Danvers, MA 01923 (telephone: 978.750.8400; fax: 978.646.8600).

ATD Press is an internationally renowned source of insightful and practical information on talent development, training, and professional development.

ATD Press
1640 King Street
Alexandria, VA 22314 USA

Ordering information: Books published by ATD Press can be purchased by visiting ATD's website at www.td.org/books or by calling 800.628.2783 or 703.683.8100.

Library of Congress Control Number: 2017941608

ISBN-10: 1-56286-786-5
ISBN-13: 978-1-56286-786-7
e-ISBN: 978-1-56286-922-9

ATD Press Editorial Staff
Director: Kristine Luecker
Manager: Melissa Jones
Community of Practice Manager, Management: Ryan Changcoco
Developmental Editor: Kathryn Stafford
Text Design: John Body
Cover Design: Alban Fischer, Alban Fischer Design
Printed by Versa Press Inc., East Peoria, IL

To the many leaders I have had the privilege of meeting over the course of my career, for modeling these truths so that I could see them for myself.

CONTENTS

INTRODUCTION

Managers have a terrible reputation. The article "Think Your Friends Have Horrible Bosses, Too? You're Probably Right" cites a survey by monster.com in which 38 percent of employees rated their boss as "horrible," and more than 50 percent rated their boss a 1 or 2 on a scale of 1 to 5. Gallup's 2015 *State of the American Manager: Analytics and Advice for Leaders* noted that nearly half of people who quit their jobs do so to get away from their managers.

You might be tempted to assume that management, as a profession, attracts annoying people. Or perhaps the nature of the role brings out the worst in otherwise kind, generous, and reasonable folks? There are more than 2 million managers in the United States, according to the latest data. Surely not all of them are horrible people. In fact, out of all the managers I have met through training programs, interviewed for articles and books, or worked with throughout my career, not one was actually trying to be a bad boss.

Most managers want to do a great job.

But obviously not all of them are succeeding.

OK, you say, maybe it's their employer's fault. Maybe they aren't trained or taught how to manage. U.S. companies spent a staggering $15.5 billion on leadership training in 2013, and that number has been growing every year since. That sounds like a lot, but when we divide it by those 2 million managers, it comes out to just over $7,000 per person.

Clearly the problem isn't that employers aren't investing at all, or that the people in management roles don't care. There's something else at work here that we need to dig a bit deeper to understand. There are some fundamental truths about management that make it hard to simply shift from a role without leadership responsibilities to one that has them—management requires different skills and habits.

In many organizations, but most notably in the IT industry, senior leadership or HR will identify someone who is a great programmer or network administrator, and put them on the management track. Here's a great contributor, they say. We need to keep her on the team. Let's give her a development plan and some incentives to become a team leader.

Think about it: What would you do if you were given the choice between taking on a leadership role or staying where you are? Most people take the promotion, even if they don't really want to be a leader. In fact, about a third of employees aspire to become managers, which is quite a substantial number. They see management as a major career achievement—the path to a higher salary and more responsibility. Some approach their promotion as if it will come with a box full of the tools they need to succeed. But when they get the new job, many don't enjoy it initially. They want to be successful, and are just as frustrated as their team members when they don't feel like they are doing it right. Studies show that less than half of managers say they feel comfortable in their roles.

What makes a great leader? Do you have to be born with some magical piece of DNA that gives you an innate ability to make people follow you? While studies have differed on which inborn traits do or don't lend themselves to leadership success, they are all in agreement that the fundamental skills of management can be learned by anyone. Management is not something you are born knowing how to do.

Bookstores (physical and virtual) are full of resources about management. There are quite literally tens of thousands of titles that offer advice and guidance on how to be a better leader, from the very short (Ken Blanchard's *The One Minute Manager*) to the very long (all five pounds of Richard Daft's *Management,* 12th edition).

Beyond the books there are magazines, workshops, blog posts, and a nearly infinite number of experts who offer even more training and resources on management techniques.

And yet. . .

Today's workforce is the most diverse in history. From the cross-cultural to the multigenerational to the global, teams today are diverse and dispersed, amplifying the challenges for leaders. Raising the bar higher still are the business pressures of cost cutting and competition. Despite the books and the training, despite the very best efforts of so many, the journey from individual contributor to manager remains a rocky road for most.

So why write yet another book about management? If the ones on the market today aren't doing the job, why add one more?

When I encountered my first management role, I was 18 years old. I had been teaching sailing in a summer program for three years when I was asked to take on the position of head instructor. My team consisted of myself and six others, all in our teens. Among them were my best friend, my cousin, and others I had grown up with over the years.

The program director was a former U.S. Air Force pilot. His first act as we launched the program in the spring was to give special jackets to the assistant head instructor, the racing coach, and me.

"You are my top three," he said, clapping us each on the back. "You are the leaders."

I was proud of my new role, and of my new jacket. You can probably guess what happened next.

My cousin and my friends immediately nicknamed themselves the "bottom four," and spent most of the summer giving me mock salutes.

Rather than being eager and willing to work as a team, they challenged everything I decided.

In response, I did everything wrong. I started issuing orders left and right. I got angry when people didn't listen. I stomped around and sulked. I was a horrible boss.

We made it through that summer, and I swore I was never going to take on a management role again. I went off to college, got a degree in psychology, and forgot all about any aspirations I might have had about leadership.

Somewhere along the way, as with most people, my career path changed. I ended up in the IT industry because I was the person who wiggled the plugs when my co-workers couldn't print. I helped people figure out how to fix things that weren't working. I taught people how to do mail merges. A few years later, I was working as an IT consultant when my manager called me into his office. The company had grown, he said, and there was an opening for a team leader. He thought I would be great.

I immediately broke out in a cold sweat.

It had been nearly a decade since my last disastrous management job. I convinced myself I would be crazy to pass up the opportunity. It can't be that bad, I thought. I've learned a lot since those days. I'll read some books and take some classes. I'm sure I'll figure it out.

Here's where I found the first problem with management training. Most of the books about management are not written by or for first-time managers. They are written by experts—experts with doctorates in motivation theory, or business executives who ran huge companies and now teach in MBA programs. These books are all interesting and valuable, but they don't get at the core of what management is all about. They are not designed to help the people who are in over their heads, trying to lead a team of their former peers, and trying to balance being a producer as well as a leader.

Over the last 10 years, I've gone from being a manager to writing and teaching about management. I do it because I truly believe that managers are the most important people in any organization. They are the ones who have the most influence on how people feel about work. Despite their reputation, almost every manager or aspiring leader I have met wants to help their team do great work.

The truth about management is that it is a skill, like any other. It takes practice to learn the habits of a leader, and to unlearn some of the habits of an individual contributor, even if they made you very successful in your previous role.

The truth about management is that there is no exact set of steps or actions that will work perfectly every time and in every scenario.

This is the story of one person's quest to become a better manager. We'll go on a journey with Julie Long as she faces a crisis just three months into her first leadership role and experiences the frustration and self-doubt that is all too common among first-time managers. Coming into her role, Julie, like many new managers, has assumptions of what management is all about. She also has habits and preconceptions about her new job that are not serving her well.

Over the course of several months, we'll follow her as she learns the core principles of successful leaders. Some of these truths come from surprising sources, but they all help her craft an authentic, strong management style of her own, as she evolves her skills and changes her approach to leading her team. Whether you are just starting your journey as a new manager, like Julie, or are more experienced as a leader, you'll likely find some parallels to your own experience.

A VERY BAD DAY

Julie trudged across the wet street, her small umbrella doing little to keep the pouring rain from soaking her suit. On top of having the worst day of her working life, she now had a long, soggy train ride home to look forward to. Checking the electronic board for her track number, she slogged over to the commuter rail and slumped down onto a wide vinyl seat. Sliding across to the window, she stared out at the rain, hoping that whoever took the seat next to her would not be looking for a chat.

Eight hours earlier, everything seemed completely different. She sighed, wondering how so much could change in just one day.

For five years, Julie had been working as a systems engineer at a large, well-known technology company. She had worked her way up from her first, entry-level position to a more senior role. Three months ago, at long last, she had been promoted to team lead. Her team was small—just three people reporting to her—but it was a big milestone in her career. She had finally made it to management.

That morning, she had gone to work filled with purpose and plans, ready for a full and productive day. Her schedule was blocked out with update meetings with her team, planning time for her own goals, and a webinar on time management. But it didn't take very long for things to start going off the rails.

Her first inkling that the day was not going to go well came as she got her first cup of coffee from the kitchen. Closing the refrigerator door after pouring in a dollop of cream, Julie found herself face-to-face with Susan, the senior member of her team, and someone who had been a long-time friend.

"Do you have a minute?" asked Susan, looking anxious and a little awkward.

Susan and Julie had met at a coding class a few years ago when they were both working to pick up a new programming language. They had quickly bonded, finding common ground in their similar approach to work. Susan was already working at Midora Systems, and when a position opened up in her group, she had emailed Julie to see if she would be interested.

For the last two years, Julie and Susan had been the senior members of the team, working closely on projects, and collaborating on innovative solutions to their clients' toughest problems. A few months ago, when the director of their group had decided the team needed a leader, Julie was given the job. Ever since, Julie and Susan's friendship had been noticeably cooler. She had hoped that things would get better, but as Susan stood in front of her this morning, Julie suddenly had a bad feeling about what was coming next.

In the small conference room next to the kitchen, Susan shuffled awkwardly, looking at the floor. "The thing is. . . ," she paused, and then the words came out in a rush. "I'm giving my notice. I've accepted another job offer, and I'll be leaving in two weeks."

Julie was floored. Susan had been with the company for nearly a decade. She was a hard worker, quiet, but always willing to put in the hours to get the job done. She was a critical part of the team.

"Why are you leaving?" asked Julie. "Is it a better opportunity? More money?"

Susan looked even more uncomfortable. "Actually it's a pay cut, but I think it's a better fit for me." She turned abruptly and opened the door. Looking back over her shoulder, she said, "I'll go talk to HR."

Julie walked back to her desk in a daze. A better fit? How could Susan feel like she didn't fit after all the years she had been there? She sat slowly, popping open her email out of habit. She had a new message from her own manager asking to see Julie in his office.

It was about to get worse.

Julie walked slowly across the hall, still trying to absorb Susan's news. As she reached her manager's office, she paused. The door was closed, which was rare.

Chuck, the director of the department, was fairly new to the organization. He had been brought in from a competitor during the last restructuring, and while he always seemed calm and competent, he wasn't the most approachable guy in the world. After her promotion, Julie had always wished she could get his advice on how to be a better team leader, but he was often engaged with other people at higher levels of the organization, and the time just never seemed right. Besides, how could she ask for help without looking like she wasn't qualified for her new role?

Julie knocked; when the door opened, she found Chuck had been talking to Magda, the director of HR.

"Come in," said Chuck, waving her over.

Magda closed the door and settled back down in her chair. Julie looked from one to the other, trying to get a sense of what was up. Chuck folded his hands on the desk in front of him and leaned forward.

"Have you talked to Susan today?" he asked.

Julie said she had, and shared the details of their brief conversation, expressing her confusion and surprise by the announcement.

There was a brief pause as Magda and Chuck looked at each other. Then Chuck sighed and leaned back in his chair.

"I guess there's no good way to say this, Julie," he said, looking down at his desk. "Susan is leaving because she doesn't like working for you. She says ever since you took over the team, you've turned into a totally different person, and she just doesn't see any future for herself here."

Julie realized her mouth was hanging open and closed it. She looked at Magda and saw her nod in confirmation.

"Listen," continued Chuck, "we all had high hopes when we recommended you for this role. You've been an excellent systems engineer, and we really thought you were prepared to step up and take the lead. I know you were excited when you took on the position. What happened?"

Running her mind back over the last three months, Julie tried to think of what exactly she had done wrong. Had she behaved differently? Of course, but that was what she was supposed to do, right? As a manager, there were all kinds of things she had to do differently.

Chuck and Magda were both looking at her.

"I guess I did what I thought I was supposed to do," said Julie slowly. "Apparently, I'm not getting it right."

Magda left, with plans to speak to Susan and see what could be done.

"Julie, I know you know how to be a great engineer," said Chuck as Julie stood to head back to her office. "But the things that made you great at your old job won't help you in your new one. Take a little time to think about what's happening, and let's talk about making some changes."

As the train pulled out of the station, Julie let out a slow sigh and wondered if "making some changes" was management speak for "getting busted back down to engineer." As she was glumly considering the prospect of failing out of her new role, a woman stepped onto the train and began walking back through the car. As she pushed back the hood of her rain jacket, Julie blinked in surprise. It was Sarah, her manager from years ago in her first "real" job. Sarah looked over and a huge smile broke out across her face. Julie found an answering, if not quite full-tilt, smile lighting up her own face, and she quickly moved her bag to the floor so Sarah could sit.

Sarah took in her soggy suit and half-hearted smile and shook her head. "Well it's been a long time since I've seen you, but it looks like this hasn't been your best day." She paused, a questioning look in her eyes.

Julie sighed and started to recount her story. She hadn't been fired, but obviously that couldn't be far away.

Sarah nodded thoughtfully. "Well you might get fired and you might not," she said pragmatically, "but if you want to be successful as a manager, it sounds like you're going to need to learn the truth about management."

Julie looked over at her, thinking maybe she had misheard. "The truth? What truth?" she asked suspiciously.

Sarah laughed, pulling out her phone to consult her calendar. "Management looks pretty easy when you're not the one doing it, but it's actually a lot harder than it seems. You can learn a lot from classes and reading books; knowing you, I'll be you've done both, right?"

Julie nodded. "I took a course last year for 'emerging leaders' but I wasn't actually managing anyone at the time."

"There are a lot of things you need to do differently as a leader," said Sarah. "It's a big transition, and it begins with your mindset about being a manager. Let's start by having coffee next week, and I'll tell you what I know."

That evening, Julie sat down at her desk and pulled out a well-worn notebook, opening it up to a fresh page. While she had been in the technology industry for her entire career, she found that spending a few minutes each day writing out her thoughts by hand, with a pen and paper, helped her relax and see the bigger picture. Sometimes it was just a few sentences or a quote that captured her mood. She leaned back in her chair, chewing on the end of her pen. It had clearly not been a good day, but she felt surprisingly hopeful. While things may still look bleak, she hadn't actually lost her job, and after talking with Sarah on the train, she glimpsed the potential of a different outcome.

Sitting forward in her chair, she wrote: The habits I have are keeping me from being successful in my new role. I'm going to need to change, which means I'm probably going to be uncomfortable.

Under that she wrote one of her favorite quotes from Theodore Roosevelt: "Nothing worth having or doing is easy."

THE FIRST TRUTH

At 10 a.m. sharp, Julie walked into the reception area of Crusher Communications. High ceilings and glass walls made the office feel open and spacious, and the walls were hung with brightly colored pictures that looked like they belonged in a modern-art museum. Sarah was waiting for her at the front, and they walked back together to a large lounge area with a kitchen.

All around them, people seemed focused and busy, working in pairs or small groups, sketching ideas on whiteboards, or leaning in to look at a design on a display. There was a constant hum of activity, but everyone who walked by gave them a smile and a quick, warm greeting.

Sarah handed Julie a mug of coffee as they sat down at a small table.

"I know this management transition has been a rocky road so far," said Sarah with a smile.

Julie shook her head, managing a wry smile. "It hasn't been one of my better moments."

Sarah nodded with sympathy. "Starting out as a new manager, there's a pretty steep learning curve. When we worked together, I'd already learned some big lessons. I've seen a lot of management styles come and go over the course of my career, but the most important thing I know about management, I learned in my first job. Maybe it will help you with your situation."

Sarah's Story

My first manager was a marketing executive named Sigmund. He had been in the advertising business for 20 years. He had been a heavy smoker early on in his life, and after he quit he was left with a voice that sounded like he had been gargling nails.

On the day I started, he sat me down in his office and gave me these words of wisdom. "Sarah," he said, "people are lazy. I like you, and I hired you because I think you have great skills. But if no one holds your feet to the fire, you'll never do your best work. I'll push you hard, and you won't always like it, but you'll do better work because I'm hard on you."

True to his word, Sigmund drove our team hard, and was all about the details. He wanted a list of what I did every day to see what I was working on. He sent back those lists, marked up with a hundred ways I could have done things better, faster, or more efficiently. He came in early, stayed late, and told me that if I wanted to get anywhere in life, I needed to do the same. I had never worked as hard in my life.

There were five positions reporting up to Sigmund, but in just two years, more than 20 people came and went in those roles. We never really got to know each other well enough to know who was working on what, and we were all so busy trying to keep our heads above water and not get fired, that we had no time to stop and chat.

One day, Sigmund left the company for another job. As the senior member of the team, they asked me to "hold down the fort" while they searched for a replacement. I'm sure you can guess what I did. With no training, and no other role models, I managed the way Sigmund had taught me. I came in early and stayed late. I demanded daily updates. I believed what Sigmund believed—that people were lazy and the only way to get them to work was to make sure they were always doing what they were told.

Just a few weeks into my new role, I was exhausted. I couldn't keep up with my own work, let alone keep track of everyone else's. I had checklists and status reports filling my inbox, and I knew that whenever I turned my back, my co-workers were slacking off or sending out their resumes. I couldn't imagine why anyone would want to be a manager; it seemed like the worst job in the world. I was so relieved when they hired a replacement for Sigmund, and I could go back to just doing my own work.

Over the course of his first few weeks, my new boss, Abraham, met with each of us one-on-one. When it was my turn, he asked me about my work. "I work hard," I said with pride.

"That's great," responded Abraham. "Do you enjoy it?"

I looked at him in shock. Was he serious? Of course I didn't enjoy it! If work was fun, it wouldn't be called work. I worked hard because that was the right thing to do, and because if I didn't work hard, how would I get ahead?

His next question was even more surprising. He asked about my goals and values, and what I knew of the goals and values of the organization. As we talked, I realized that unlike Sigmund, Abraham didn't believe we needed to be pushed hard to be productive; he believed that we would work hard to do things that matter to us. If we cared about the goal, Abraham believed we would find creative and efficient ways to achieve it.

Over the next two years, my feelings about work changed completely. Sure, I had been proud of working hard when Sigmund was my manager, but I never had any idea what I was actually accomplishing by completing all the disconnected tasks on my never-ending to-do list. Working for Abraham was very different. We met each week as a team to talk about challenges and opportunities. We knew how our different roles fit together to move the team and the organization forward. Everyone on the team knew that we were working together to do something important.

Julie stirred her coffee thoughtfully. While she hadn't been as much of a dictator as Sarah's first boss, she realized that she also hadn't spent much, if any, time talking about the bigger picture of the team's goals. She had been so focused on not dropping the ball on any of their deliverables that everything she talked about revolved around daily tasks and getting things done.

"It sounds so easy when you put it like that," Julie said. "But how do you actually do it? How did Abraham get you all on the same page?"

"One way that works for me is to create a team vision," answered Sarah. "We have a company vision and mission statement, and then as a team, we create one of our own that describes how the work we do every day helps achieve those goals. Why don't you come sit in on a meeting and see how it works?"

Julie agreed, and she and Sarah headed into a nearby workroom. Like the rest of the office, the collaboration space was bright and open. There were markers all over the tables, and the whiteboards and flipcharts were filled with ideas and sketches from previous meetings.

On the far side of the room three people were clustered around a monitor with a website mock-up on the screen. Sarah introduced them as Marco, Jeremy, and Casey—members of the design team who had been working on a website project for a startup for the last month. Marco was project lead, Jeremy was coding the site, and Casey was creating the illustrations and visuals. After these quick introductions, the team turned back to the monitor and picked up the thread of their discussion. It seemed that they had shown the mock-up to the client, and even though everything they had put together was exactly what their contact had asked for, the founder of the startup didn't think it represented the spirit of the organization.

Marco was frustrated. All the content had come from the client, and between the three team members, they had built out the design based on several hours of meetings with the client's marketing director. They had sent over concepts and mock-ups in the last few weeks, but because of his schedule, the CEO hadn't reviewed them until this last version, when things were very nearly final.

"We've put in more than 80 percent of the hours we allocated for the project, and we did it based on the information we had from their marketing lead. If we have to start from scratch, we'll completely blow out the project budget," said Marco, sighing heavily.

Julie and Sarah listened as the team considered their options. They could replace the visuals, and see if that changed how the CEO felt. They could start from scratch and insist on his involvement, and come up with an estimate of how much it would cost to redo the process. Or, they could hand over what they had done to date and suggest the client find another designer. No one really liked the third option, but there seemed to be no way to finish the project on budget and still make the client happy.

After a few minutes of discussion, Marco went over and wrote a sentence on the whiteboard. It read:

At Crusher Communications, we help our clients tell their story to the world.

Underneath that he wrote another sentence:

The web design team collaborates with people who aren't technology experts, to help bring their story to life through beautifully designed and thoughtfully built web-based solutions.

The team stood back and looked at the vision statements together. Marco turned to the team and spoke.

"I think we need to ask the CEO to meet with us. It's our job to help them tell their story, and if he doesn't believe what we've created does that, then it's up to us to find out why. We won't have to recode the whole site, but we will probably have to put in a few more hours than we originally thought to update the visuals and adjust the content."

Marco looked at Sarah.

"Are you OK if we spend a few extra hours on this project?"

"Of course," Sarah said and smiled. "And I would be happy to be in the meeting with the CEO if you think it would help, but I think you're making a good decision that supports what we are all trying to do here at Crusher."

With that settled, the team went on to discuss other projects. Sarah and Julie stepped back out into the lounge area.

"Well," asked Sarah, "what do you think?"

"I think I have a lot to think about," answered Julie. "We do have a company vision, but I'm not sure I could write it down for you off the top of my head. I know we don't have a team vision, and I can definitely see how useful it is to have something to look to for guidance. I've also realized that I've been spending too much time focusing on the daily tasks, and not enough time helping my team understand why we do what we do."

"Then you've discovered the first secret about management," Sarah said. "There are a few more though, and here's someone I think you should meet."

Sarah handed Julie a business card. She looked down at the small piece of paper in her hand. It said:

Mike Rogers
Field Supervisor
Miller and Sons Construction

"Construction?" Julie looked at Sarah in surprise. "I'm leading a team of software developers. What can a construction manager teach me?"

"Why don't you go ask him?" said Sarah with a smile.

That evening, as Julie sat down with her journal to reflect on her day, she flipped to a completely empty page and wrote:

THE TRUTH ABOUT MANAGEMENT

Vision: Define the values your team shares and measure everything you do against those values.

CREATING A VISION

The first thing Julie did after coffee with Sarah was go straight to her company's website to look up the organization's vision statement. There it was, right on the About page:

> At Midora Systems, we believe that software should be intuitive, reliable, and secure, so our clients can focus on what they do best.

As she read the statement, she recalled the CEO making an announcement earlier in the year about how all the initiatives in the organization were organized around the core values that their customers had shared in a recent survey. While she had been at the all-staff meeting for the announcement, Julie had been focused on a tight deadline and hadn't really paid attention to what that vision statement might mean to her or to the team she worked on. This was several months before her promotion, but it had not occurred to her to revisit the company vision as part of transitioning into her new role.

After seeing how valuable the vision statement was at Crusher Communications, she realized that she couldn't recall a single time she had considered these larger objectives in the context of her own team's goals. Rather than proactively aligning their activities, Julie realized they were more often working in a reactive mode, rushing from one project to the next.

She wondered how Sarah and her team found time to think about the team vision and aligning their goals. While everyone had seemed busy, they also seemed to operate with a strong sense of purpose. Even though it had probably taken some time up front, it was clear that the benefits of having that shared vision were substantial.

Just then a calendar reminder popped up, announcing that the weekly team meeting was due to start in 15 minutes. Julie gathered up her laptop, and, with the seed of an idea taking shape in her mind, headed over to the conference room.

Stepping into the meeting right on time, Julie was met with a familiar sight. All three of her team members, Susan, Jamal, and Bryce, were seated around the table with their laptops open, busily responding to emails and updating project status notes. Before her visit with Sarah, Julie thought she would have been happy to see everyone working so hard. But with her new insights into the value of shared vision, she realized that despite all the activity taking place, there was no clear sense of progress, just stress and busyness.

Calling the meeting to order, Julie asked everyone to close their laptops and put away their phones.

"I know we typically use our weekly meetings to give updates on our projects and activities," Julie began, "but today I'd like to do something a little different."

As she looked around the table she saw a range of responses to her change in agenda. Susan, no doubt still anxious about the response to her announcement this morning, looked dubious, perhaps wondering if Julie planned to share the news with the team. Bryce seemed curious. Jamal sat back with his arms folded and brows furrowed, uncertain how to respond to this change in routine.

Julie took a moment to write the company vision statement up on the whiteboard. She then asked each team member to list the initiatives that were currently on their plate. After all three were done, Julie stepped back from the board to take a look. As she considered the volume of activities that the list represented, one thing was absolutely clear.

"There is more work here than we can deliver effectively," said Julie.

Looking around the table, she could see an even mix of relief and skepticism. Susan shook her head, frowning.

"Of course there is," Susan said. "There is always more work than we can possibly do. It's frustrating because we can never catch up, and we can't do our best work when we're always so busy."

Julie nodded. "I agree with you. What I'd like to do today, rather than reviewing all the things we're working on, is to think about what we do best as a team, and how our work helps the whole organization. Then let's see whether what we're working on matches up well with that vision, or if we should take some things off the list. I'd like to start by thinking about two things."

She stepped back up to the whiteboard and wrote two questions at the top, above their list of activities:

- What is the most important thing our team does in relation to the company vision?
- Which of our projects are most closely aligned with that thing?

At first the team was cautious, hesitant to throw out ideas. But once they had a few things on the board, opinions and ideas began to flow quickly. As a team, they were writing the code for several new features that would be included in the next version of the software. Together they began to form ideas of a statement that brought together the key ways they added value to the process.

While Bryce and Jamal were the most vocal at first, Susan began to chime in more and more often. Julie took notes, creating a document filled with everyone's ideas and concepts. After 15 minutes of animated discussion, they had created a short list of ways their team's work contributed to the goal of building intuitive, reliable, secure solutions that kept their customers focused on their own work.

After a few more minutes of discussion, they were able to separate the project list into three distinct categories. There were three core initiatives that aligned directly to the goals of their team, and to the organization as a whole. Another five initiatives were categorized as important, but not as urgent as the top three. They had also identified four things that were taking up time and energy, but weren't clearly aligned with any goal.

Making a note of the four initiatives that didn't fit, Julie turned back to the team. Their meeting time was nearly over, but she had one more question to ask.

"I know we're all working hard," she said, looking around at each person in turn, "and I know sometimes it can be frustrating. But I'd like to take a minute and go around the table and hear from each of you why you do this work. Why did you take this job, and what do you really enjoy about it?"

For a moment it was quiet, and then Bryce answered.

"I like creating new things. It's the most fun for me when I can figure out a way to solve a problem that no one has thought of before. I feel like every day is a little different, so I never get bored."

Jamal shook his head. "I have always liked to make things work. That's why I stay in this same role." He looked over at Julie. "No offense, but I never wanted to be a manager; it's a headache to have to tell everyone what to do all the time. I like being really good at what I do, knowing I can make things work when other people can't."

Susan smiled reluctantly at Julie. "I do enjoy managing projects. I like knowing the technical side, but also working with people to understand what they need and to come up with the pieces they don't even know to ask for. I like helping people."

The pieces were all coming together for Julie. "I think we're all here for the same reason," she said. "We're good at what we do, we care that the products we create are top notch, and we want the people who buy them to get exactly what they want and need, even if they don't know how to ask for it."

As she ended the meeting, Julie told the team that she would work with Chuck to either eliminate or reprioritize the four projects that they had identified as out of alignment with their goals. Everyone agreed that without those items, they would not be so stretched and could focus on delivering a great result for the other initiatives. As they left to head back to their workspaces, Julie could feel the positive energy. Bryce and Jamal were engaged in an animated discussion about the pros and cons of a content management platform, and Susan seemed at least reluctantly positive.

Knowing that one good meeting didn't mean everything was fine, Julie headed back to her desk to think about what else she could do. While understanding their shared values would certainly help Julie prioritize their work, she still felt like she was missing some key factors in how to be a better manager. When she was a developer, she had always known exactly what she needed to do every day. Like Bryce, she enjoyed the challenge of solving new problems, but she didn't seem to be able to get a handle on exactly what she was supposed to do as a manager.

She looked at her calendar—just like her team, she felt busy all the time. It was rare that she had a chance to sit back and think strategically, and when she did have extra time on her calendar, she wasn't sure exactly what to do with it. Typically, she would end up pitching in on a project; at least she felt productive doing that.

There was clearly more to the management role than she understood. Opening her email, Julie found a note from Mike Rogers, the construction manager Sarah had mentioned. He invited her to visit his work site the next morning at seven. Feeling a little skeptical about what she could learn from someone in a totally different industry, Julie hesitated, but she trusted Sarah. She wrote a quick reply, accepting the invitation, and then set her alarm for 5 a.m. so she would be ready in plenty of time.

THE SECOND TRUTH

The first rays of the sun were just touching the treetops as Julie pulled into the visitor's parking section at the construction site. Grabbing her coffee from the cup holder, she stepped out of her car and waited as several large pickup trucks rumbled past. Looking out across the site, she could see cranes in motion lifting lengths of steel up to the highest floors of the half-finished building. At ground level, bulldozers were smoothing out a space that she thought might one day be a parking lot, and she saw the building interior light up from the sparks of the welders' torches. It was 7 a.m., and while her own workday wouldn't start for a couple hours, things here were well under way.

Crossing the lot, Julie followed the signs directing her toward the field office. As she came to the door of a trailer, a big man in a yellow hard hat stepped out toward her. He wore a safety vest and brown canvas overalls, and had a radio on his hip. He looked exactly like her mental image of a construction foreman, so she stuck out her hand.

"I'm Julie. Are you Mike?"

He stopped and shook her hand.

"Duane Robinson," he said. "Are you looking for Little Mike or Big Mike?"

"Mike Rogers," answered Julie.

A huge grin spread over Duane's face. "That's Big Mike, the supervisor." He tapped his yellow hard hat. "Big Mike's hat is white. He's inside the trailer."

He jerked his thumb at the door and walked briskly toward the construction zone, tossing a casual "have a good one" back over his shoulder.

Julie gave a mental head shake. She had no idea that the different hard hat colors meant anything. She had always worked in office buildings full of cubicles and conference rooms. She was so used to the norms of that environment that she felt like a fish out of water in an unfamiliar industry.

Stepping into the trailer, she stopped again, taking in the blueprints on the walls, the desks pushed into the middle of the space, and the maze of folding chairs. A young man with dark hair and glasses was standing behind one of the desks making notes on a yellow pad. He looked up as she entered the room.

"You must be Julie Long," he said, smiling and stepping around the desk to shake her hand. "I'm glad you could make it this morning."

Julie smiled, and then looked puzzled, recalling what Duane had said. "Are you Mike Rogers?" At the young man's nod, Julie was about to ask about the Big Mike nickname, because he seemed not only younger, but several inches shorter than Julie herself. But before she could ask, the door to the trailer swung open and a man stepped into the space.

"We've got a problem, Mike," he said without preamble, brows drawn together, and a deep frown creasing his face.

Mike turned immediately and greeted the man with a quick smile. "What's up, Enrique?"

Julie, still trying to get her head around how things work in this environment, turned to listen. Enrique had on a green hard hat and was wearing a heavy leather jacket over the rest of his clothes. His long, gray hair was pulled back into a ponytail and held with a bandana. He was describing a complex issue related to how one of the specialty tools they used for welding had broken down.

Mike listened intently, asking detailed questions as Enrique explained the situation.

"What do you think is the best way to deal with this today to keep things moving forward?" asked Mike.

Enrique scratched his head and then, unexpectedly, started laughing. "Well, we can always do things the old way for today while we send the equipment out for repair."

Mike nodded. "I'll make some calls and we'll get things in motion this morning. Thanks for bringing it to me."

Enrique headed for the door. "Do what you do best, man," he said.

Mike turned back to Julie and apologized, saying he needed to make a few quick phone calls. He was back a few minutes later, jotting a quick note on his yellow pad before popping on his hard hat and handing one to Julie.

"I have to ask," said Julie, wondering how to frame the question. Mike anticipated her, grinning.

"How old am I?" he said with a laugh.

"Yes!" said Julie. "That guy has to be 20 years older. Why is he coming to you when he already knows what to do?"

"It will make more sense when I tell you a little bit about how I ended up with this job," said Mike. "Let me tell you my story."

Mike's Story

My dad was a heavy equipment operator. When he immigrated to the United States from Brazil, he was only 16 and barely spoke English, but he had a talent for working with machines. If it had a motor, he could make it work. He always had an engine that he was fixing in the basement. He started off doing landscaping work, and then learned to drive a skid steer. After a few years of that, a friend who worked in construction asked him to join the team, and he learned to drive backhoes, excavators, bulldozers, and finally a crane. His new boss helped him get certified, and as he worked his way up, he started making a good living.

My parents married when they were very young; Dad was 22 and Mom was 20. She was working at a coffee shop, and he would stop there every morning on the way to work to get his coffee and donuts. Just a year after their first date, they got married, and less than a year later, I was born.

I spent a lot of time around construction sites when I was growing up. My father would bring me to work with him on Saturdays and let me touch the trucks, climb up on the treads, and sit in the seats. I loved the huge machines, but my mother always wanted me to stay in school and go to college.

My first job in construction was as a laborer. I worked every summer from the time I was 16, going onto the job sites with my dad. He worked the heavy equipment, and I did basic labor jobs. I spent an entire month handing bricks to a mason. I spent another summer running errands and picking up supplies. It was hard work, but I got to see every aspect of how construction works. I met so many people like my father, who had worked for decades as welders or electricians or crane operators. Each one knew more about their job than I did. But I saw something else, too.

Even though each person on the site was an expert, none of them could actually build a whole building by themselves. Every expert is necessary, but someone has to coordinate all those individual experts for the whole job to get done. So, I started paying more attention to the guys in the white hard hats, and I saw how they fit into the picture.

I worked for some really great bosses and some really lousy ones over those years. One year we had a foreman who told the crane operator to double up on the load because he had promised the client that we would be done a week early, and things had to move faster to meet that schedule. He and the operator got into a huge argument, and the operator walked off the job because he knew what the foreman was asking wasn't safe.

There was another year when the owner of the site would show up and want to hurry up one particular part of the job, even though he didn't know anything about how parts fit together. He would call the drywall contractor and tell them to come a week early and get started, even though the electricians and the plumbers weren't done with their work. It made everything harder.

I worked for one foreman, though, who really stood out in my mind, and he's the reason I'm here today. He was a quiet guy, but he was always listening. He walked around the site and saw for himself how things were going. When someone came to him with a problem or a question, he asked lots of questions instead of simply giving an answer. He respected the knowledge that each person on the site brought to the job, and he always asked what they would do to solve the problem. Sometimes he would bring in people from other parts of the job and see if they saw another way to solve the same issue. He'd listen to both and then figure out the best solution.

Everyone on the job respected him, and everything just seemed to run more smoothly on those sites. Problems got solved quickly, and we were almost always ahead of schedule.

I went to college, but I still worked construction in the summers. I got my degree in engineering just a few years ago. I've been offered office jobs away from the field doing design work, but I love what I do here. I understand how all the pieces fit together. I won't ever be as great a welder as Enrique, or as good a crane operator as Duane, but I know that what I do is really important. I solve problems so the women and men on the job can focus on what they do best. I see the big picture, and I make sure everything fits together.

While Mike was talking, he and Julie walked across the site. While everyone at her office pretty much looked like they were doing the same thing (sitting at a desk, typing on a computer, talking on the phone, or sitting in a meeting), everyone here was doing something visually different. A woman with a walkie-talkie was coordinating the placement of a beam with the crane operator. An electrician was wiring a series of outlets on the ground floor. Everywhere people were working independently, each one moving the whole, complicated plan forward.

Everywhere he went, Mike was greeted with a quick wave or a "hey Big Mike." Sometimes he stopped to take a look at something or ask a question, but Julie could see that he was absorbing all the activity and comparing it to his big-picture vision of what should be happening.

They headed up a level on a freight elevator, and Mike called over to Enrique, whose team was working on the second floor. Spotting Mike, Enrique flipped up his welding mask and cocked an eyebrow.

"Did you do your magic?" he asked.

"I found a rental, so we'll be all set this afternoon," responded Mike. "The broken equipment is going to be picked up in an hour, and then we'll have the temporary one by 2 p.m. today."

Enrique gave Mike a thumbs up and a big grin. "That's what I'm talkin' about!" he called, and then flipped his mask down and bent back over his project.

Walking back to the trailer, Mike finally answered the question Julie had been embarrassed to ask.

"I'm 29," Mike said, smiling. "Some of these men and women have been on the job since before I was born. I always know I'm not the most experienced person in the room, but I also know that I don't need to be."

Julie nodded, beginning to see why Sarah had suggested she come talk to Mike.

"I've always felt like I have to know everything about everything," she said. "I'm worried that if I don't know something, the people on my team will think I'm not competent to lead the team."

Mike shook his head. "There's no way you can know everything. When I was in college I took a business class and the lecturer wrote this quote from Steve Jobs on the board:

'It doesn't make sense to hire smart people and then tell them what to do. We hire smart people so they can tell us what to do.'

"I always remembered that," Mike went on. "It just seems to make so much more sense, but it's obviously not what every company or every manager does. In our industry, everyone has to be a specialist, and that means focusing on their area of expertise to the exclusion of everything else."

He paused, chuckling.

"I remember a day when one of the drywall contractors didn't show up. We asked one of the masons to pitch in because we were under a deadline and needed an extra pair of hands. Boy, was he a fish out of water. Everyone gets used to being the expert in their own area, but when you're asked to do something different, you realize how much skill is required to do a job that might look easy from the outside."

Julie nodded. "We have that problem, too. Everyone thinks if you're in 'technology' that you can do everything from writing code to fixing servers. The truth is that almost every role is specialized. If you're on the management track, your technical skills get rusty and it's hard to go back."

"From what I've seen, what makes a great manager is someone who's naturally curious about how things work," said Mike. "They understand that things are complicated, and even though they can't necessarily do every job themselves, they are familiar with the terminology. They know how to ask questions and really listen to the answers. I think what builds trust is being willing to listen and try to understand."

Julie made a mental note to look up the Steve Jobs quote and put it up in her office. She turned to Mike and thanked him for all his advice.

"I learned something I never realized today," she said. "The manager's job is to see the big picture and make it easier for the team members to do what they do best."

Mike nodded. "I never really thought of it that way, but it's true. I don't think of myself as a manager; I think I'm an obstacle clearer." He chuckled. "Maybe that's just because I always think of things in construction terms."

Julie smiled back, and then had to ask the question that had been nagging at her since she'd met him. "Hey, why do they call you Big Mike?"

Mike grinned again. "When I started working in construction, there was a guy on the site who was six foot four and had to weigh close to 250 pounds. He was a mountain of a man. His nickname was Little Mike. He was a friend of my dad's, and when I started coming around the site, he would always call me Big Mike for fun. It just caught on. It's a good reminder that people aren't always what you expect them to be."

When they reached the trailer door, Mike and Julie shook hands, and he handed her a business card. Julie looked down, assuming it was his, but seeing a different name, she looked at him with a raised eyebrow.

"My sister-in-law is a manager at a company that builds online training programs," explained Mike. "She works out of her house, and runs a team that's spread out all over the world. You said you work in

IT, so I'm guessing you have people who work remotely, too. She won an award at her company last year for leadership. Give her a call—I bet she has some ideas for you."

Julie thanked him and headed for the visitor parking lot, still trying to absorb what she had seen and learned that morning.

Back in her car, she pulled out her notebook, opened it up to the page she had started after talking to Sarah, and wrote another line.

THE TRUTH ABOUT MANAGEMENT

Vision: Define the values your team shares and measure everything you do against those values.

Team: Know your team members' strengths and focus on clearing the obstacles to their success.

Satisfied, she pulled out her phone and looked at it for the first time since she had arrived an hour before. She could tell right away that something was up. She had turned her ringer to silent for her trip to visit Mike, but her screen was lit up with notifications. A client had left her two voicemails, and she had a flood of instant messages from her team, her boss, and one of the other team leads. With a knot in her stomach, Julie began to read through the messages. When she had listened to the client calls and skimmed through the IMs, it was clear that one of the team's most critical projects was going off the rails. She maneuvered the car onto the highway, calling Susan to get a status report.

5

AT LEAST IT'S NOT RAINING

As she drove back to the office, Julie thought about the situation, which she had pieced together from reading through her emails and IMs. Last week, one of their key clients had been upset that they couldn't pull data directly from the Midora application into their financial system. While Midora was compatible with several other major software packages, the one this client was using wasn't among them. The sales team had come to Julie for a piece of custom code that would allow them to connect the Midora application.

Susan had written the code, but she hadn't been happy about it. She had warned both Julie and the sales manager that the reason they didn't support this financial system was because it was older, used different protocols, and had the potential to corrupt data in transition. But the sales team insisted that it was critical to keeping the client on board.

"Our website says our system integrates with leading financial systems," she remembered Marcus from sales saying in his email to their group, including Julie's manager and the VP of software development. "We need to make this happen or we're going to lose a six-figure deal."

So, Julie had asked Susan to write the code despite her concerns. Antonella, the team lead for one of the integration services groups, had her team test it and install it on-site. Everything had seemed smooth for the last two weeks, but this morning the client's entire system was down, and no one on the client site could access the financial system. It was a nightmare. The client's CEO had called CEO of Midora, and everyone in the company was on high alert.

<hr />

Too impatient to wait for the elevator, Julie sprinted up the stairs to her floor. She popped out of the stairwell and stopped to catch her breath in the reception area before hurrying down to her team space. She could see the voicemail light on her phone blinking madly, and the team conference room was full of people. Without stopping to check her phone, she headed straight into the fray.

Susan and Bryce were hunched over a laptop, clicking through lines of code. Antonella was on her cell phone listening and taking notes. Julie spotted Jamal at the other end of the table and headed over to sit next to him. He looked frazzled.

Julie's stomach lurched. No wonder Susan looked ready to spit nails. If Julie had listened to her a few weeks ago and pushed back harder, this wouldn't be happening. It was just this kind of scenario that had caused Susan to get frustrated and go looking for another job.

Antonella hung up the phone and came to the table.

"We've got a tech heading over to the client site now," she said, her expression grim. "I'm hoping he can roll back the code change and get them up and running, but they've already lost at least half a day of work, and the issue is affecting their customers."

Julie stepped up to the end of the table and looked out at the two teams. Susan was still hunched over her computer scowling at the code, Jamal was doing his best to disappear, and Antonella was pacing. Everyone was tense. Taking a deep breath, Julie spoke.

"I know we would all like to turn the clock back, but we don't have that option. Right now we have to get things fixed for the client, and then make a plan for how we're going to move forward." She paused, looking around at the anxious and aggravated faces in front of her.

"I'll go upstairs and brief both Chuck and the CEO, so they are in the loop. We'll need to keep them up-to-date on our progress, and they are going to want to know exactly how this happened." Julie paused again, looking down at the table. Then she focused on Susan.

"Susan, I know you tried to tell me that this was going to be a problem. You were right. I should have listened and pushed back harder on the sales team so they understood the risk we were taking on this."

Susan nodded, and then gave a wry smile. "At least they can't fire me, because I already quit."

Julie and Antonella both chuckled, and the mood lightened a little. It was true, but to Julie, it still felt like a low blow because she couldn't imagine how she would solve this problem without Susan on the team. Her absence was going to leave a big hole in just a few short weeks.

Julie headed upstairs to the CEO's office. Murali Raman had launched Midora Systems after his previous startup was acquired by Google. He was brilliant, a perfectionist, and everyone walked on eggshells around him even on a good day. Today was not one of those days.

At least it's not raining, thought Julie as she knocked on his door. She found her own boss, Chuck, already sitting at the small table in Murali's office, along with Maria Lopez, the VP of sales. All three of their heads swiveled toward the door as Julie entered, and for a moment she seriously considered turning around and heading down to Starbucks to see if they were hiring. Taking a deep breath, she walked into the room, prepared to go to bat for her team.

The next half hour was one of the hardest of Julie's career. Maria was frustrated that Julie hadn't made the risks more clear (although Chuck did point out that even if she had, the sales team still would have wanted to go ahead because the customer was insisting on the integration). Murali grilled both Chuck and Maria on why they hadn't brought this decision to him.

"I never want to get a call from the CEO of one of our clients claiming that our product is preventing them from doing business," he said, slapping both palms down on the table. "Our customers have to be able to trust that we make their operations better, not worse!"

Julie suddenly had a realization that made everything clear in her mind.

"Our vision is to make software that's easy to use, reliable, and secure so our clients can focus on what they do best," she said, quoting from the vision statement she read a few days earlier. "In this case, we were trying to say yes to the client, even though we knew what we were doing wasn't consistent with the vision."

She hadn't really meant to say it out loud, but as she looked up, she found all three executives looking at her thoughtfully.

"I think there's a disconnect between our team and the sales team," she went on slowly. "We want to help, but sometimes even when we know things aren't going to work out we think we can't say that because, even though we say the customer experience is what matters, everyone knows the only thing that's important is hitting the sales numbers every quarter."

Maria frowned. "We don't try to push the envelope all the time. We know that signing a bad deal isn't good for the company. But maybe in this case Marcus was too concerned about hitting his quota and didn't really try to understand why your team was pushing back."

Julie paused and then—figuring that since she had gone this far, she might as well say the rest—she continued.

"This situation happened because I didn't do the right thing. If we're going to avoid this sort of scenario, I need to do a better job helping your team understand what we're concerned about, and I need to do a better job of understanding the issues the salespeople are dealing with. I'd like to suggest that the sales team, the integration team, and my team meet as a group and come up with some better ways to share information."

Maria was nodding, and Chuck gave her a quick smile. Just then a text popped up on her phone from Susan that said, "They're back up."

Julie gave a deep sigh of relief and shared the news with the rest of the executive team. They weren't out of the woods yet, but at least the client was able to do business again.

Chuck and Julie walked out of Murali's office together. "I know this hasn't been an easy week for you, but I think you made a great point," said Chuck. "This isn't the best time for more drama on top of Susan giving her notice. And I don't mean to add stress to your plate, but I'd like to see a plan for how you're going to approach the changes we talked about. It seems like you've got a new perspective on things lately."

Julie nodded, wishing she had figured out exactly what she needed to do. The conversations with Sarah and Mike had helped, and she was beginning to see how she needed to change her mindset and her approach, but she hadn't yet put it all together. She knew it was going to take a while to absorb all the information, and it was hard to focus on trying to be a better manager when fire drills like this could happen at any moment.

Chuck stopped at his office door and turned to look at her. "Do you know why I recommended you for this job?"

Julie shook her head.

"Because you care about what happens." He paused to let that sink in. "Do you know how many people show up for work and are just putting in their time? It's a lot more than you'd think. It can be stressful to care about the quality of the work, to care about the clients, and to care about the people on your team, but it's what will make you a great leader once you get your feet under you.

"I also appreciate that you took accountability for the problem just now," continued Chuck. "That takes some nerve, especially in front of the CEO."

As he turned and headed into his office, Julie walked down to the kitchen to make herself a cup of coffee, thinking about what he had said. It was true that every manager she had ever really enjoyed working for was someone who had a passion for not only the work, but the people. They were people who put in the extra effort to get things done right, and people who took the time to get to know you as a person, not just an employee number. She knew she still had a lot to learn, but as Julie took her coffee back to her desk, she felt more optimistic than she had for a long time.

She pulled out the card for Mike's sister-in-law, and sent off a quick email introducing herself and asking if they could set up a time to chat.

6
THE THIRD TRUTH

O ver the next few days, Julie and her team worked to sort out the
leftover issues from the client crisis and keep other projects on
track. Susan's departure was coming up quickly, and Julie's nights were
spent reviewing resumes and trying to find someone who could fill the
gap. Susan's skills were unique, and finding someone who could do all
the things she could, as well as gel with Bryce and Jamal, was going to
be a big challenge.

With everything that was going on, she was surprised at how quickly
her appointment with Carolina, Mike's sister-in-law, came around on
her schedule. Julie had planned to work from home that day, so she
would be able to ask questions without worrying what other people in
the office thought.

Their meeting was scheduled for 1 p.m., so after a morning of focusing on her own work, and a quick break for lunch, Julie opened the
videoconferencing and screen-sharing link that Carolina had sent her.
She was instantly connected to a smiling, curly-haired woman sporting
a pair of retro cat-eye glasses with rhinestones on the rims. Carolina
fairly bubbled with energy, and Julie found herself smiling back, her
own energy level rising to match.

Carolina started off by giving Julie a quick overview of her five-person team: two graphic designers, two instructional designers, and a software developer. Together they worked to build out online courses for clients, ranging from how-to style videos to fully immersive simulations. Working out of her house in Maine, Carolina managed a team that had never been in the same location at once. Three of her team members worked out of their homes in the United States—one on the West Coast, one on the East Coast, and one in Texas—one of the graphic designers lived in Thailand, and the other, a digital nomad, was currently exploring Alaska.

"We never know where Nikki is going to be," said Carolina, laughing. "She spent a year traveling through Europe and she was in a different country almost every week. As long as she has Wi-Fi, she can work."

While Nikki was the only member of the team who traveled full time, everyone on the team had a flexible schedule, and it was rare for anyone to work a standard eight-hour day.

"How do you all stay on the same page if you don't work at the same time, and you're never in the same room?" asked Julie.

"We use a lot of collaboration tools, and we make sure we always know who is responsible for each deliverable," responded Carolina. "We all have specifically defined roles on the project, and my job is to make sure that the goals and timelines are really clear so people can plan their work without holding up anyone else. We focus on the results, not on how much time anyone spends at their desk."

"I was always taught to focus on the inputs, not the outputs," said Julie. "One of my first managers told me that if you're doing all the right things, the good results will follow."

Carolina nodded. "That's true to a point. There are habits you should certainly have that will make you more successful over time, but focusing too much on inputs can turn you into a micromanager, and nobody likes working for one of those!"

Julie laughed and nodded her agreement. There was nothing worse than working for someone who wanted to tell you how to do your job.

"What do you do to focus on results?" asked Julie. "I try to set goals with my team, but then things get busy and those goals fall off the map because of a client crisis or a change in priorities. It's hard to figure out which results are truly going to matter in the long run."

"That's true, too," Carolina replied, "I always try to build in time to put out fires, so that they don't completely throw us off schedule. We use the Eisenhower Grid quite a bit as a tool to make sure we're focusing on the right things."

"The Eisenhower Grid?" asked Julie, eyebrows raised. "As in President Eisenhower?"

"That's the one," laughed Carolina. "Basically it's a time management strategy." She pulled up the virtual whiteboard on their shared screen and quickly sketched a box divided into four quadrants. She drew an arrow pointing up the side of the box and wrote "urgent" next to it. Then she drew another arrow pointing from right to left, and wrote "important."

Labeling each square with a number, she began to explain.

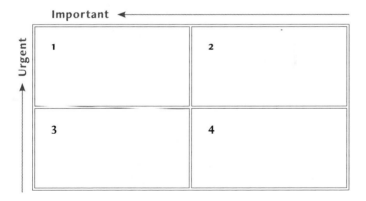

"Things in the first quadrant are both important and urgent. They are the things we have to get done every day, and they almost always get done because they have a high priority." She pointed at the box labeled with the number four.

"Things in this quadrant are not important and not urgent," she continued. "Honestly, these are things we shouldn't be spending any time on. We try to take a look at any tasks that end up in that box and acknowledge that they are a bad use of time. Sometimes it's a bad process that's wasting people's time, or something a client is asking for that's out of scope and nice to have, but not really part of the project.

"Those two quadrants are pretty easy. The harder ones are number two and number three," continued Carolina, using her cursor to shade those two quadrants orange. "A lot things like professional development, strategic planning, and other proactive work falls into quadrant two. It's really important stuff, but it's always getting bumped off of the daily schedule by things that are more urgent."

Carolina paused and pulled up her calendar to show Julie how she had blocked out several half-days in orange. "These are times I've set aside to do the things that fall into this second quadrant," she said. "Sometimes I use it for one-on-one meetings with my team or to work on improving our tools and templates so we can be more efficient."

Julie nodded thoughtfully. "That's a great idea," she said, pulling up her own calendar. "I feel like those meetings are the first thing to get pushed off the schedule when an emergency comes up, though."

Carolina smiled. "That used to happen to me, too, so now I've made a rule that I can't write over them without moving them to a new slot. That way if the time has to get pushed, it doesn't get lost completely!"

While Julie's team typically worked together in the office on a regular basis, she could see how a lot of the tools and processes Carolina used could help make things more efficient.

"It seems like you have some really good ways of staying organized and in communication," said Julie. "How did you convince your company to let you operate completely virtually? Don't they put pressure on you to come to the office?"

"Well it's not always easy," laughed Carolina. "Let me tell you the story, and then I think it will make more sense."

Carolina's Story

Growing up, I always loved art. I drew pictures everywhere—on my notebooks at school, on the back of receipts, on my mom's grocery lists. I was always making things into art. I was raised by a single mom. She was an incredibly practical person, and she negotiated with her boss so that she could work from home in the afternoons. I grew up seeing her balance work with being a parent, and I don't think I ever really understood how hard she had to work to make that happen. It was in the days before we had all these collaboration tools and resources, so she brought home stacks of paperwork, and she would spend hours on the phone.

When I was thinking about what I wanted to do for work, everyone told me that making a career as an artist was impractical. My guidance counselor at school suggested that I choose something like accounting or engineering because there were always jobs in those fields. She suggested I keep my art as a hobby.

Lucky for me, the Internet completely changed the opportunities for artists. While I was still in college, companies began understanding the importance of a web presence, and by the time I graduated there was a thriving opportunity for graphic designers to create everything from web-based marketing materials to products like games and online courses. I was thrilled to be able to do what I loved as an actual job.

However, I quickly realized that creative work doesn't always work the way the working world does. Sometimes I would get great ideas in the middle of the night, and I would stay up all night working and be exhausted the next morning. I also didn't feel inspired working in a cubicle in an office. Sitting in traffic for an hour just to get to my job sucked up all my creativity, and I found myself sitting at my desk feeling miserable.

Over time I learned what works for me. I have a couple of hours first thing in the morning where I can dig down into a project and really focus. Then I need to take a break—go for a walk, throw in the laundry, do something that has nothing to do with work so I can get my energy back. In the afternoons I can have calls or online meetings, and do a lot of collaborative work, but around three or four I feel like my energy has just dried up, and what I really need is a nap. At eight or nine at night, I often come up with a great idea, and sometimes I'll stay up late or be totally focused on something that inspires me for a couple of days straight.

I thought I was the only one that worked like this, because I had spent several years working in smaller organizations where I was the only one doing design and artistic work. But as I began to network with other designers, I found that lots of people felt like the way they worked didn't fit into the Monday to Friday, nine to five schedule. Some of them were artists like me, others were parents like my mom. There were people from all different walks of life with all kinds of goals for how they wanted to integrate work with their lives.

It really clicked when a friend sent me an article about Nathaniel Kleitman's research. A physiologist who specialized in the study of sleep, Kleitman observed that people have a regular rhythm, not only to their sleep, but to their energy levels during the day. I started to spend a lot of time reading about how our bodies work, how our brains work, how people are motivated, and the creative cycle. For the first time, I didn't feel like I was weird for being more productive and more efficient when I chose my hours.

With that said, I knew that the key to working the way I wanted was all about being clear about what I was producing, rather than where I was sitting. I knew that I needed to be able to show that I was able to collaborate and get the job done no matter where my office was located or what hours I worked. It took some time and quite a bit of trial and error, but I found it comes down to two things: clear, consistent communication and well-defined goals.

Carolina paused to make sure Julie was taking everything in.

"I know this sounds like a lot, but we use two acronyms to help us keep on track. The SMART framework helps us make sure every goal on our team is designed to be:

- **Specific.** We write up a detailed goal description for each project element.

- **Measurable.** Every goal has a clear finish line or way of defining when it's successfully completed.

- **Achievable.** I make sure the team member and I both agree that they have both the time and the tools to get the job done.

- **Relevant.** No one likes to do busy work, so we check every goal to make sure it relates to our core project goals and objectives.

- **Time bound.** Every goal we create has an end date.

"That's just one way that we use goals to keep track of what we're doing and hold ourselves accountable to getting the job done, no matter where we are. The SMART model isn't new, but it's a good place to start. GRASP, the other acronym I like to use, goes beyond just creating the goal and gets into what you need to get it done.

- A **goal,** which conforms to all the elements in the SMART framework, is the baseline.

- **Resources** are what you need to achieve the goal. I use this to help my team think about what they need from me or from the organization to get the job done.

- The **action plan** is what you put together to make sure you've thought through all the steps and know what you need to do every day.

- **Support** is what you need from management to make sure that other groups will collaborate with you when you need them.

- **Purpose** is how the goal ties into the larger vision of the organization. It's last on the list, but it's one of the most important factors to consider.

She paused to take a breath, laughing. "I'm guess I'm a little bit of a goal-planning nerd, but I've always felt like I could do my best work as a manager by helping people break things down into bite-sized chunks and then figure out what they need to do to get those things done. It works really well for me and for my team."

Julie had always used goals in her own career development, and while she had set goals with her team members, she began to see that just having a goal wasn't enough. The key was in both the structure of the objectives, and their alignment with the vision.

She recognized the inherent truth in the concept that people are motivated differently. She knew Jamal, Susan, and Bryce were excited by different things, but that hadn't translated into the work they were assigned, or into any flexibility in terms of how they might like to work. She recalled a management article a friend had sent her about the role of choice in motivation and decided to dig that up and reread it. She also realized that many of the objectives she had for herself and for her team members didn't pass the SMART test.

"I've learned so much in the last few weeks, and you've given me so much more to think about," Julie said. "I thought I understood what it meant to be a manager, but there's a lot to it that I never recognized."

Carolina smiled. "I know I'm not a perfect leader, but here's what I know. Everyone needs to have a clear vision of what they need to do every day, and the tools to do it. Whether your team is spread out across the world like mine, or sits together in one room, they still need clear goals, and know what they need to do to achieve them."

That idea made complete sense to Julie, who had always been a goal-oriented person. But she also could see how those goals could tie back to the vision. After signing off her virtual session with Carolina, she opened her notebook and added a new entry to her growing list of truths.

THE TRUTH ABOUT MANAGEMENT

Vision: Define the values your team shares and measure everything you do against those values.

Team: Know your team members' strengths and focus on clearing the obstacles to their success.

Goals: Focus on the outputs and recognize each successful achievement.

7

GETTING TO THE WHY

The morning train into the city the next morning was full. Sharp-dressed businesspeople with briefcases and laptops sat side by side with medical professionals in scrubs and comfortable shoes and construction workers in boots and hard hats. Julie typically spent the ride observing this wide variety of individuals. She and her brother had often taken the train into the city when they were growing up to visit museums or to meet up with their father for a quick lunch break. To pass the time, they loved making up stories about the people they saw in the seats around them, imagining astronauts and spies, brain surgeons and senators, all heading off to their busy offices.

Today, Julie barely saw the people sharing the trip. Her attention was completely captured by an article a friend had sent her on motivation. It reminded her of the conversation she had with Sarah just a few short weeks ago about her managers Sigmund and Abraham. This piece drew from recent research on motivating creative work, and it proposed a strong argument for how people are motivated as well as a framework for leading creative teams.

The centerpiece of the article was a four-part grid describing how to evaluate motivation issues. The horizontal axis was labeled "can" at one end, and "can't" at the other. The vertical axis showed "will" at the top, and "won't" at the bottom. In each section of the grid, the authors described the applicable motivation challenges and how to resolve them.

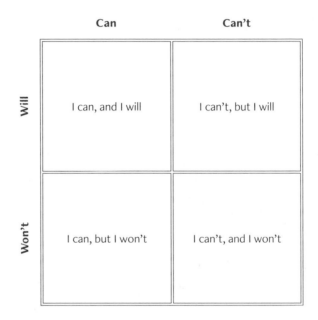

Quadrant one was green and labeled "I can, and I will." According to the article, these employees are in some ways the easiest to manage. They are high performers, strongly self-motivated, and highly skilled. The challenge is keeping them excited and motivated, removing any barriers they face, and providing them with the tools they need to be successful. It sounded easy, but as Julie read the section, she knew that this was where Susan had been just a few months ago, before Julie took over the team; now she was on her way out the door, taking her skills and strengths to another organization. Shaking her head and wishing there was more detail on the topic, Julie scrolled to the next section. Rather than moving to the second box, the authors skipped to the red box in quadrant four.

"I can't, and I won't," read the headline. The question that immediately popped into Julie's head was reflected on the page: How do these people get hired? Typically, if team members are in this quadrant, they are a bit of a lost cause. Whether they got here through burnout or fell through the cracks of the hiring process, people who don't have the skills they need to do the work and aren't willing to make the effort to learn are a significant liability on the team. Julie nodded to herself—while neither Bryce nor Jamal fell into this category, she had certainly seen and met people like this during her career. It was always frustrating because it meant everyone else had to make up for their lack of competence.

Skipping down to the next section, Julie began to read about quadrant two: "I can, but I won't." Here, the authors asked: Have you ever had a team member who has all the skills to be successful, but just doesn't seem to want to do the work?

Julie found herself nodding again. Unlike the previous sections, the article went into far more depth on this quadrant. While it's easy to place the blame for lack of motivation squarely on the shoulders of the team member, it's much more likely that this situation has come about through poor management. Julie's eyebrows went up at that, but reading on, she realized that she had felt this way on several occasions.

Company culture plays a significant role in whether talented people feel like they can do their best work. And on a day-to-day basis, the direct manager of a highly skilled individual can have a strong influence on whether that person thinks it's worth the effort to do a great job. There are a variety of reasons great people become unmotivated, the article went on. Inconsistent recognition and compensation programs are often at the root of motivation issues, but it's not always about money or even about being appreciated. In many cases, smart people are frustrated by barriers to their ability to do their best work; one of the most common barriers is time.

The authors of the article proposed imagining for a moment that you are a painter. You are hired based on a portfolio of work you created over a long period of time, with careful attention to detail. You've shared your very best work, and you know that you are capable of capturing a certain lifelike quality of light in your subjects. Now imagine that you are asked to paint the same exact painting, 20 times a day. We've all experienced the frustration of continuously being asked to do more, to do it more efficiently, and to eliminate errors. While driven by good intentions, this workplace philosophy can be seriously aggravating to creative professionals, and that's not just artists and writers. Our workforce is full of people who create solutions rather than manufacturing widgets. Yet we have not always adjusted our management practices to account for the differences in how creative people are motivated.

Julie paused in her reading, struck by how on-the-mark these observations were. Developing software was almost never a matter of cranking out code by the hour. She had felt that sensation in the pit of her stomach when she knew that there just wasn't time to do the job right. Knowing that what you created would be incomplete or buggy was incredibly demoralizing, yet in many cases that was the only option, given tight timeframes and competing priorities.

As the train pulled into the station, Julie tucked her tablet back into her bag and walked off the platform toward her office deep in thought. She had weekly update meetings scheduled today with Susan, Bryce, and Jamal, and she knew what needed to be on the agenda.

First up was Susan, and while this was technically a weekly update, with just a few days left until her last day, the atmosphere was markedly different from their previous meetings. For one thing, Susan was smiling. For the last few months, every meeting with Susan had felt like a tug of war. She was obviously frustrated, and Julie had felt like she couldn't change any of the things that made Susan unhappy. But new insights from both the conversation with the CEO and the VP of sales, as well as the article she had just read, had led Julie to an epiphany, and she started the meeting by sharing it with Susan.

"I know it's too late to change the fact that you're leaving," Julie began, "but I wanted you to know that I've started to recognize some of the things I've been doing that have made your job harder. I never knew that, as a manager, my job was not just to pass down the initiatives and goals that came from the other groups and the leadership team to you guys, but that I also needed to push back on what we can and can't do successfully as a team. I've been allowing it to be a one-way flow of information and objectives, and now I can see that it created a really frustrating situation for you and for the team when I agreed to goals and targets that we couldn't successfully achieve."

Susan nodded. "I knew you were trying to figure out all your new responsibilities, but it didn't help when we were always being asked to do more, and it wasn't ever possible to do the work successfully. It feels like we've been doing nothing but putting out fires for months. It's been exhausting."

Thinking back to the article she had been reading on the train, Julie realized that Susan was a great example of someone who had been in the "I can, and I will" quadrant, but because she couldn't see any way to be successful, her motivation had been eroded to the point that she felt like doing her best work wasn't getting her anywhere. Julie could see that it wasn't just a single event, but a series of frustrations that had led Susan to this point, and she said as much.

As Susan gathered her things and headed back to her desk, Julie walked to the kitchen to grab a cup of coffee before her meeting with Bryce.

Bryce had been a bit of a puzzle for Julie since she took over leadership of the team. When they had been peers, before Chuck tapped Julie to lead the group, she and Bryce had been pretty close friends. Outgoing and charismatic, Bryce had been the social leader of the group. At least once a month he would send out emails suggesting they meet for drinks after work or take a team outing.

When Julie took on the leadership role, she had started declining his invitations to socialize, figuring that she needed to draw a line between her personal and professional lives. It just didn't seem appropriate to hang out at the bar with people that she was supervising. While she still felt like that was the right decision, she missed some of the camaraderie that came with those casual outings.

There was no doubt that Bryce was talented. He absorbed information like a sponge, seeming to pick up new programming frameworks and languages easily. Where Susan was a steady, patient worker, Bryce was a ball of energy when his attention was captured by a new challenge. He would send Julie emails at 2 a.m. or on Saturday, excited to share how he finally solved a problem. But he also had a tendency to procrastinate, especially if he found a particular task to be boring. Confident to the point of being cocky, Bryce could always pull out the work at the last minute, but if there wasn't a looming deadline, his productivity would often drop off a cliff, and Julie found herself nagging him for updates, pushing him to finish the simplest things.

He seemed to fall into the "I can, but I won't" category, and as Julie came back to her laptop with her coffee, she considered what she might be able to do to move him into the "I will" quadrant.

Bryce entered Julie's office and dropped down into a chair with a grin on his face.

"So when Susan goes, I'll be the senior person on the team, right?" He put his elbows on the table and leaned forward. "I bet you're planning to give me a big raise, too!"

He looked so pleased with himself that Julie couldn't help laughing.

"I don't know about a big raise," she countered, "but I do want to talk about your goals, and what the future might hold for you."

Bryce sat back and cocked his head to the side.

"Well, now that sounds interesting. What did you have in mind?"

Julie picked up her mug and took a sip of her coffee as she marshalled her thoughts. Since reading the article that morning, and reflecting on Susan's reasons for leaving, she had come up with an idea, but before she could put it out there, she needed to know some things from Bryce first.

Julie stepped up to the whiteboard and drew a line from top to bottom, dividing the board in half. On the left side she wrote "Motivates" and on the right she wrote "Frustrates."

"Let me ask you something," she began. "What makes you excited to come to work?"

Over the next 15 minutes, they filled up both sides of the board.

Motivates	Frustrates
• solving tough problems • learning new things • working with smart people • getting things done • money	• stress • boring stuff • people with no sense of humor • my old crappy laptop • doing the same thing every day • not enough time off

They sat back and looked at the list together.

"If you could change one thing about your job," Julie asked, "what would it be?"

Bryce rubbed his chin and looked at the list.

"Well the easiest one on the list is a new laptop," he said, giving her the side eye.

"Consider it done," Julie responded. "What else?"

Bryce reviewed the list again.

"It's funny," he said, shaking his head slowly. "My whole career I've felt like money was really important. But when I make more money now, it just doesn't seem to make as much of a difference to how I feel about my work. I'd rather be learning new things, working with smart people, and maybe have a little more time off to travel."

Julie thought it was time to introduce her idea.

"How about this," she said, opening her laptop. "I'll go to bat for you on the laptop, the time off, and a training budget. But there's something I need from you."

Bryce looked at her and cocked an eyebrow.

"We need to bring on a new hire, and I have to decide whether we're hiring someone at Susan's level to fill the gap, or if we can hire someone more junior who can grow into a great team player." Julie paused and looked across the table at Bryce. "I'd rather hire someone who can grow into the job, but I need to know that you can step up and be 100 percent reliable, even with the boring stuff."

She could see that Bryce knew exactly what she was talking about, and she saw him weigh it up in his mind. He could get some of the things he wanted, but he was going to have to put in the extra effort to make it happen. She picked up her coffee mug again, only to find that it had gone cold while they were talking.

Julie gave Bryce a moment to absorb all the information they had just discussed. She didn't want to push him to make the decision. Her coffee refill could wait; having Bryce on board was an important part of making this plan work. After a few moments, he stood and extended his hand across the table.

"I'm in," he said. "Shake on it?"

They shook hands, and she went for her refill of coffee with a smile spreading across her face.

With one more meeting to go, Julie felt like she had made progress. In some ways, she figured her last one-on-one would be the easiest.

Jamal had been with the team for just over a year. He was a career-changer with kids in high school, and in many ways his personality was the polar opposite of Bryce. Julie smiled wryly to herself as she recalled Jamal's first week. At the end of every day he had turned to her solemnly and said, "It was great working with you, Julie, thanks for everything. I'm pretty sure I'm getting fired tomorrow."

It was only partly a joke. Jamal was one of those people who seemed to attract bad luck on projects. If something could go wrong, it would.

But, Julie had always admired Jamal's tenacity. Even when things went wrong and even if he was never sure he could solve the problem in front of him, he never gave up. He just kept plugging away, doing his best, and worrying that it wasn't good enough. Unlike Bryce, Jamal never avoided the boring stuff. He was a steady performer, and he didn't complain about much of anything.

Popping open her laptop, Julie quickly recorded what she and Bryce had written on the whiteboard, and then erased everything except the top headings. She was curious to see what Jamal would come up with if she asked him the same questions. According to the article she had been reading that morning, Jamal probably fell in the "I can't, but I will" category. He didn't always have the skills or the confidence to get the job done, but he was always willing to try.

Jamal knocked on the doorframe, peeking in through the open door to make sure Julie was ready for him. She looked up with a smile and handed him a whiteboard marker. Quickly describing the exercise, she posed the same question to Jamal she had posed to Bryce.

"What makes you excited to come to work?"

Jamal sat down, turning the marker over in his hands as he considered the question.

"The truth is, I'm not excited to come to work most of the time," he said slowly. "It's not that I don't like my job, it's just that 'excited' is the wrong word. I don't like to be excited at work, actually. I like to come in and know what I need to do, and then get it done." He looked at Julie with a small smile. "I guess you know I don't really like surprises. I like things to be predictable."

Julie nodded. "That makes sense, and it's something I appreciate about your approach," she said. "You're the most reliable and consistent person I've ever worked with. But what I would like to understand today is what makes you feel motivated, as opposed to what makes you feel frustrated with work."

Julie and Jamal talked through his experience with work, and after about 30 minutes, the whiteboard was full.

Motivates	Frustrates
• understanding expectations • good project management • clear communication • knowing how to do a good job • being told that my work helps and is important to someone	• changing priorities • fire drills (not the facilities kind) • not knowing who's making the decisions • having to "wing it"

The first thing that struck Julie as she considered what Jamal had shared was how different it was from what Bryce had written. While they both disliked stress generally, they defined it in very different ways. Where Bryce was enthusiastic and excited by change and challenges, Jamal wanted a more stable environment. Where Jamal loved process and clarity, Bryce preferred to figure it out as he went along. Both were strong contributors to the team, but in their own ways.

Julie filled Jamal in on her idea about hiring someone more junior to the team, rather than replacing Susan with someone else at that level.

"I've asked Bryce to help take on some of Susan's responsibilities," explained Julie. "I'd like to ask something else of you, too."

Jamal looked worried, and Julie knew he was thinking she might ask him to jump into some of the more complex client issues. These were exactly the type of scenarios that stressed him out, and while she could see that he wasn't happy about it, as usual, his answer was positive.

"OK, what can I do to help?"

Julie smiled.

"I depend on you to be a stickler for documentation and process. I'd like you to take over the documentation and project management process and make it as clear as possible." She paused, noticing that Jamal was suddenly looking a lot less nervous. "I'd also like you to mentor our new hire on our processes as a team. Is that something you're willing to do?"

A full-blown grin broke out across Jamal's face.

"I can absolutely do that," he said with relief.

With her meetings wrapped up for the day, Julie headed back to her desk feeling like she finally understood something about management that had eluded her up to this point. While she couldn't control the work that came to the team, she could definitely make it less stressful by playing to each person's strengths, rather than asking everyone to do the same work.

Back at her desk, she found an email from her father inviting her to a football game over the weekend.

"I know you've been trying to figure out some things at your job," the note read. "I'd like to introduce you to a guy who might be able to help."

Julie felt her eyebrows go up. A guy at a football game was going to help her become a better manager? A few weeks ago she would have sent a polite "thanks but no thanks," but over the last few months she had found surprising truths about management in unexpected places. Why not at a football game?

THE FOURTH TRUTH

It was a perfect day to watch a football game. Bright sun shone down from a clear blue sky, and the air was crisp and cool. The glare of the sun temporarily blinded Julie as she came out of the tunnel and into the packed stands of the stadium. Shielding her eyes, she looked up at the stands and caught sight of her father, Paul, standing and waving at her. She headed up the steps to meet him.

Paul was a tall, lean man in his mid-60s. An attorney by trade, he had exchanged his courtroom suit for a sweater and a leather jacket, and his short black hair was covered by a red-and-white-striped hat topped with a pom-pom. A baseball player in his youth, Paul still carried himself with a natural athlete's grace, and his eyes sparkled with excitement, as they always did whenever he watched a sporting event.

Julie had never been particularly coordinated and preferred hiking or jogging to team sports, but she had always watched football and baseball with her dad. His enthusiasm was contagious; whether they watched in person or on TV, she could count on him to stand up and cheer when his team scored, and to cover his face and groan at every setback. He was a relentless optimist, and no matter how lopsided the score got, he would watch the game until the last second ticked off the clock.

"It's going to be a great game," he said, turning to lead her through the row to their seats. "I want to introduce you to a good friend of mine, Coach Marcus Parker."

Marcus stood as Julie came down the row, and reached across to shake her hand.

"Marcus was one of my best friends in college," her father said, settling himself into his seat. "He's a partner in our firm, but when he's not in the courtroom, he's coaching youth football."

Julie sat down next to Marcus and looked at the field. The teams had just finished the coin toss and were getting set for the kickoff.

"Who are we rooting for?" asked Julie, turning to her father. He pointed to his hat.

"The guys in red, of course!"

Turning to Marcus, she asked if that was his team, too.

"Well neither of them are my team," he responded. "I just love the game. I've been playing since I was a kid." He gave Julie a side eye and a smile. "You could say that I owe my life to football."

Intrigued, Julie cocked her head. "I'd love to hear about it if you're willing to tell me."

Marcus's Story

I was always a big kid. My mom used to say that when I was born I skipped right over the baby clothes and went straight to size 2. She had all these cute clothes she wanted to dress me up in, but she had to save them all for my brother. In school, I was always in the back of the class pictures because I was taller than everyone else.

Lots of kids think it's good to be big—that it means you can stand up for yourself and no one messes with you, but that's not true. When you're the biggest, sometimes people want to knock you down just to prove something. I was shy. I didn't make friends easily, and I spent a lot of time by myself.

My mom was worried about me. My dad was in the army, and he was often deployed overseas when I was growing up. We lived in a tough neighborhood, and she had seen kids get into trouble on the streets. When she saw I was spending so much time alone, she knew she had to do something, so she signed me up for the local football program. At first I thought it was a terrible Idea. I didn't want to go out on the field and hit people. I thought football was just pushing and shoving.

But by the end of my first practice, I could already see that wasn't the case. My coach was a natural teacher who loved the game and taught us to love it, too. We learned about hard work, but we also learned about life. We learned how to work as a team, and how to support one another.

I played football all through school. I never thought I would go to college, but my coach talked to my mom and told her I had a good shot at getting a scholarship. There was no way I could have afforded to go if it wasn't for that money. It changed my life. I have a great job and I make a good living, but I wouldn't be here if I hadn't learned to love the game of football from that first coach.

Julie smiled at Marcus's story. "I guess I don't know enough about the game. I still just see a lot of pushing and shoving going on. Maybe you can tell me what I should be looking at."

Marcus chuckled. "Well in the first place, you've got to put together a great team. No matter how well you design your plays, they won't work if you don't have the right people to get the job done. Football is all about knowing your team's strengths, and finding the plays that help you make progress."

He gestured at the field as the quarterback passed the ball off to the running back, who bulldozed forward for a few yards.

"You watch. They tried a run play there and it didn't work. Now they'll try a passing play. For the first few minutes of the game, they'll try every kind of play to see what the defense does to stop them. They're testing and learning to see what works."

Julie thought that sounded strangely familiar. She had come to the football game to take a break from thinking about management, but this sounded a lot like good advice for running a team. Curious to see if the parallels held up, she turned to Marcus.

"How does it work?" she asked.

Marcus pointed down to the sidelines.

"During the game, the coaches are calling the plays. They decide what the players should do in each situation, and the players are doing just what they've practiced. Where they are standing at the snap, where they run, what they expect the other players to do, all of those elements are designed and practiced during the week. They become like tools in a toolbox. Out on the field on game day, the coaches call the plays they think have the best chance of beating the other team."

Julie nodded, peering down at the man in the hoodie and heavy coat striding back and forth on the other side of the field. He was watching the team intently, and at every break in the action, he flipped through a binder full of photographs and diagrams. Occasionally, he would jot down notes and speak rapidly into his headset. He was so focused on the game, Julie thought a herd of elephants could be stampeding by, and as long as they weren't on the field between him and his team, he wouldn't even notice them.

"Once the game is over, the whole coaching staff shifts into learning mode," continued Marcus. "They look at the video of the game moment by moment. They see what worked, and what didn't. They see who did their job, and who was in the wrong place or doing the wrong thing. During the week, they work with individual players on skills, and they work as a team practicing plays until everyone knows exactly where they need to be in every situation."

Julie nodded. "I've just started to realize how important it is to think about the different roles we have on our team."

On her other side, Julie's father was standing and waving his hands.

"Intercepted! I can't believe it!" he shouted. "Why did he throw the ball there? There was no one even close! It was nothing but guys on the other team and now they've got the ball back."

Collapsing back down in his seat, Paul groaned. Marcus chuckled.

"Every game has its ups and downs," he continued. "In my whole career I've never seen a perfect game. Even the most talented people make mistakes; that's just human nature. It's unrealistic to think that there won't be any errors or miscommunications, but you get better by looking at what happened, learning from what went wrong, and trying to find ways to improve." Marcus shook his head. "The fans always want perfection. They want everything to work just like it's drawn up on the whiteboard. But there are always surprises. There's just no way to predict what's going to happen on the field."

Julie smiled. "That sounds a lot like what happens to us at work. The sales team wants every customer engagement to be perfect. They hate mistakes, and whenever we have one, it seems like it's the end of the world. But every project comes with its challenges."

"In football, we can review the videos and see what we did," said Marcus. "What do you do on your team to try to look back and learn from some of those challenges?"

"We should debrief after every project," acknowledged Julie, "but it doesn't always happen. We're so busy trying to get on to the next thing that we often don't get to those meetings, and if we do, we don't always go into the issues in depth."

Julie thought about the meeting she had with Maria, the sales VP, a few weeks ago. She wondered how much they could learn if they held debriefs, not just within her own team, but with the sales team as well.

"We talk a lot about hiring people with a 'growth mindset,'" Julie said thoughtfully. "We send people to technical training, and we have other programs to help people grow their coding skills or their project management capabilities, but I don't think we spend enough time looking at the actual work we do from day to day, and learning from that."

Paul jumped up out of his seat again, this time to cheer for a 35-yard touchdown pass.

"Big plays like that are always great when you can pull them off, but the truth is, the game should never come down to making a throw like that," commented Marcus. "The work you do to gain ground, keep the ball moving, and get first downs is the heavy lifting that wins games. It's about discipline."

Julie nodded, finding more similarities between Marcus's approach to coaching football and her management challenges.

"How do you handle different personalities on the team?" asked Julie. "I only have three people to worry about. Well, four if you include me. There are so many more personalities to think about on a team this big."

Marcus nodded. "It's tough sometimes. You can get some big egos on a football team, that's for sure. People think every game is all about them. But, what's important is that everyone has a job to do, and while those jobs are all different, they have to come together to achieve the one purpose we all agree on, and that's winning football games."

Julie told him a bit about her time with Sarah, and the idea of a vision. She mentioned her conversations with Mike and with Carolina as well.

"I've learned a lot in the last few months. I guess when I took on the management role, I thought it was all going to be about telling people what to do and having them do it." Julie laughed. "That almost never happens in the real world."

Marcus smiled. "The truth is that leadership comes down to a few essential elements." He ticked them off on his fingers. "You have to really care about people and want them to succeed. You have to like a challenge and not get frustrated when things don't always go your way. And you have to get back up and try again when you get knocked down."

Marcus turned toward her to emphasize his last point. "As the leader, you need support, too. Even the coach needs a coach sometimes. Don't work so hard on developing your team that you forget to develop yourself."

After the game, Julie walked with her father and Marcus back down through the stadium and out to the parking lot.

"You've given me a lot to think about," said Julie. "And not just about football."

"Keep learning every day," said Marcus, shaking her hand.

Julie gave her dad a quick hug. "Thanks for inviting me," she said with a smile. "I learned a lot about football."

"I knew you would," responded her father with a grin. "Marcus is a smart guy."

Julie nodded, wondering how much her father realized about her work. He often seemed so focused on his own world, and had certainly only seemed to be aware of the game today. But Julie also knew that he always saw beyond the obvious, which was what made him so successful as an attorney. He had a reputation for being hard as nails, but Julie knew he was secretly a softy at heart, especially where his kids were concerned. Chuckling at his subtle approach, she headed off to her own car.

On the ride home, Julie thought through what she had heard. She kept coming back to the idea of focusing on learning. While it was something they talked about all the time, she had always thought of it in the more technical sense—taking classes, getting certifications, and gaining skills. But the more she thought about it, the more it seemed like she was missing an opportunity for her team to learn from each other, and to get better every day.

Back at home she dug her increasingly dog-eared journal out of her work bag and flipped it open to the page where she had been keeping a list of what she had learned about management. Under the heading "The Truth About Management," she wrote the fourth truth.

THE TRUTH ABOUT MANAGEMENT

Vision: Define the values your team shares and measure everything you do against those values.

Team: Know your team members' strengths and focus on clearing the obstacles to their success.

Goals: Focus on the outputs and recognize each successful achievement.

Learn and Adapt: Develop the habit of learning from each day's work and focus on growth, not perfection.

LEARNING IN THE
TRENCHES

Balancing her coffee mug on top of her laptop, Julie headed over to the conference room. After the last week's client debacle, she decided to schedule a debrief meeting with the team. But first, she wanted to talk to Maria and Antonella.

Reflecting on her meeting with Murali, Chuck, and Maria, Julie realized that thus far she had only been doing half of her job (and even that not very successfully). She had been focused on getting the team to do what she wanted them to do, but she hadn't thought about her colleagues or the other departments her team partnered with to deliver on the larger vision of the company. After the disastrous day last week, the importance of that partnership process was very clear.

Stepping into the conference room, she put her laptop down and turned to greet Antonella.

Working directly with customers as part of the integration team for nearly a decade, Antonella had a warm, engaging personality and a wide smile. Originally from Jamaica, she stood nearly six feet tall, with long braids cascading past her waist. She still retained a hint of an accent from her years living on the Caribbean island, and while she loved her job, she was roundly critical of the winter weather and had been especially irritable this month, as the last of fall had slipped away and the snow had started to pile up.

Maria came in soon after. A graduate of Harvard Business School, she had been heading up the sales team for the last six months. Like Chuck, she had been brought in during the reorganization to reboot the sales division. Smart and aggressive, Maria had designed a sales pitch and process that had doubled their monthly sales revenues in just a few months, and her goal was to continue that trajectory.

While Antonella was easy to talk to, Julie found Maria incredibly intimidating. But after last week, she knew she had to try to work more closely with both of them, as well as their teams.

"Thank you both for taking the time to meet," began Julie. "I know we have been working side by side for a while, and while we do a pretty good job handing things off through the sales process, there are obviously times when things fall through the cracks." She paused, with a nod toward Maria. "Your team is really crushing it on the sales side, which is great for the company, and we want to be able to support that growth. I think going forward we're going to need to do more than just work side by side, so I thought we could start with opening up the lines of communication among the three of us."

Maria nodded thoughtfully. "That makes sense to me. Anything we can do to eliminate obstacles to our growth is something I support. What do you suggest?"

Julie opened her laptop and pulled up a document she'd created listing the challenges she saw on her end, but before she could suggest that they brainstorm the challenges, Antonella spoke up.

"I agree, too. Before Chuck came on board, the development and integration teams were merged. Julie, you probably remember that time, but Maria, it was before you arrived. We decided to split up the teams because we didn't want the developers out in the field doing integration. It's a different skill set." She paused and grinned at Julie. "Don't take this the wrong way, but I picked my team for their ability to work with people, not their ability to write code."

Julie acknowledged the dig with a smile, knowing that Antonella wasn't being critical. It was true that the skills required to be on the integration team were different than those she looked for on her own team. She remembered what it had been like when she was required to go into the field and try to help get clients up and running. It hadn't worked well, and was frustrating for both the clients and the engineers. The decision to create a separate team to work with the clients during the installation process had been a smart one. But it also meant that there were now three separate groups involved with onboarding a new client: Sales had to convince the customer to buy the product. Integration had to get the client up and running and help them learn how to use the software. And development had to continually improve the product based on client feedback, as well as changes in technology infrastructure.

While all three groups reported up to the CEO eventually, Maria, Antonella, and Julie were basically peers, without any reporting hierarchy among them. But Julie realized that they also held the same shared values and vision that drove the whole organization.

Julie stepped up to the whiteboard, and wrote the Midora vision at the top. Underneath that she began to write down the challenges she had put in her notebook the night before.

"I know we won't solve everything today," said Julie, "but I think it makes sense to start off by talking about where we each see obstacles or challenges that keep us from working together as well as we need to."

They talked through a variety of issues, from salespeople inventing imaginary features because a client asked for them to developers failing to understand how annoying a particular bug was from the client's point of view. Julie was glad they had started the conversation with just the team leaders, as she knew her team members would have taken some of the comments personally. Mentioning that thought out loud, she got a resounding agreement from both women.

"Actually," said Maria, "this reminds me of what happened in my last job. It's something I think we should be thinking about as leaders. We want our teams to be able to have debriefs and learn from mistakes, but that's harder than it sounds. At my last job we had a really toxic company culture. It was incredibly competitive. The leadership team would single out anyone who made a mistake, and that person was held up to the team as an example of what not to do. One of my colleagues referred to it as the 'invisible gun.' If you were the one that screwed up, and the invisible gun was pointed at you, your whole goal was to find a mistake that someone else had made so that the heat would be off you, and on to someone else."

Maria shook her head, sighing. "We tried to pretend that it was a great culture," she continued. "We called it 'intense' to our friends, and made excuses about how we were all getting toughened up. But the reality was that many of us were very unhappy. On top of that, it was never about learning from those mistakes; it was just supposed to be a deterrent so we would all try harder next time. But if you don't really look at what you're doing and share information, it doesn't matter how hard you try, you'll never be 100 percent perfect."

With a wry smile, Maria looked at Julie and Antonella. "I'd like to build a different culture here, and I'd really appreciate working with both of you to do it." She turned to Julie. "When you took accountability for the client blow-up last week, I was surprised and impressed. I was falling back to my old habits of trying to find someone to blame. It made me realize that we can choose not to have that culture here."

Antonella was nodding. "I have worked in places where everyone just kept their heads down and hoped they didn't get in trouble. I don't want it to be like that here. On my team, we have a weekly 'mistake meeting' where anyone can share something they think they didn't do right or want to try to do differently next time. It works because we trust that no one is going to tear another person down for admitting they did something wrong. It may take some time to build that trust across all our teams, but I think it starts with the three of us."

As they wrapped up the meeting, they agreed to schedule some team collaboration time to each take the most pressing challenge on their team's list and come up with some recommended solutions. As she left the meeting, Julie felt like she had taken a big step forward.

As she walked back to her desk, Julie pulled up her email and saw Magda had sent her the job description they were about to post for Susan's replacement. Opening the attachment, she skimmed through the description. After her conversation with Jamal and Bryce last week, Julie had sent a draft job outline up to Magda requesting a more junior resource to hire onto the team. Based on the document she had just received, Magda had changed it back to a higher-level position that looked more like a clone of Susan.

Julie sat back in her chair, slowly rereading the posting. She pulled up her original email to Magda, just to make sure she had sent the right document originally. Printing both out, she considered her next move.

Clearly Magda didn't think the lower-level hire was the right answer. Julie had good reasons for wanting to hire at a different level, but maybe she hadn't made that clear. Not a big fan of confrontation, Julie didn't like to get into arguments and sometimes felt flustered under pressure. But in this case it was clear that Magda wasn't respecting her decision as team leader. She had three choices. She could give in and let Magda post the more senior role, but after her conversations with Bryce and Jamal last week, she knew that wasn't the right solution. She could also go to Chuck, and hope that he would deal with Magda.

Heaving a deep sigh, Julie chose the third option. She needed to meet with Magda directly and stand up for her decision. Before she headed over to Magda's office, Julie gathered her notes. She put together a quick summary of her reasoning, the commitments from Jamal and Bryce, and the draft onboarding plan she had created for the junior resource she was expecting to hire. She sent off a quick email to Magda confirming that she was available to chat, and then straightened her spine and headed in to fight for her team.

Magda's office was bright with early afternoon sunlight. Head down, studying a resume, she glanced up as Julie popped her head in the door, and waved her over to a chair. Julie waited as Magda finished her notes, and then when she set aside the paper, Julie put the two job descriptions on her desk.

Magda looked up and arched an eyebrow.

"Is there a problem?" she asked.

Julie slid the more senior job description forward toward Magda.

"Yes," she answered. "I recommended we hire a more junior resource, but it looks like the job description you've sent is for someone more like Susan."

Magda nodded.

"I did see your job description, but don't you think we ought to get someone in who can fill the gap Susan is leaving? We've got a lot of initiatives that depend on your team's capabilities. It makes more sense to me to hire someone more senior."

Julie felt frustration bubble up, and had to pause to push her emotions back down. She knew that getting aggravated would not bring Magda around to her point of view. She laid out the facts, explaining the balance of skills on the team, her analysis of Bryce's and Jamal's strengths, and her strategy for onboarding the new team member. She walked through the job description she had written, showing Magda how this resource fit with the team's needs, but also gave them room in the budget to bring in contractors with specialized skills when needed.

Magda leaned forward, brow furrowed.

"You make a good case," she said, running her finger down the bullet points on Julie's onboarding plan. "I still think you should consider hiring someone at a higher level though. Let's bring Chuck into the conversation and see what he thinks."

"Actually," Julie interjected, "Chuck already approved the job description I wrote. He was copied on the email."

Caught by surprise, Magda gave a short laugh and looked at Julie with approval.

"This is a bit of a backhanded compliment," said Magda, "but you've come a long way in the last few months. I didn't think you had put real thought into this, but you've put together a solid plan here. Since you and Chuck are on the same page, I'll post your version, and we can get started screening candidates."

Walking out of Magda's office, Julie let out a long breath and felt the tension drain out of her neck. She had gone to bat for her decision and it felt good. As she walked past Chuck's door, she paused, and then poked her head in to ask if he had a minute.

Bringing him quickly up to speed on the conversation with Magda, she told him they were going to go ahead with bringing in candidates, and hopefully would have someone on board soon.

"Sounds great," said Chuck. "I'm glad you popped in, I have been meaning to ask you about something else as well."

Rummaging through a pile of cards on his desk, Chuck pulled one out of the stack and handed it across to Julie.

"Alicia Stone," said Chuck, pointing at the name on the card. "She's a management coach I met recently at a conference. I really liked her, and I thought you might like to give her a call to see if she might be a good resource for you as you continue to grow into your role. I have some space in the training budget, and rather than taking another course, I thought you might prefer to work with a coach."

Julie looked down at the card.

"I've never worked with a coach before," she said. "How does it work?"

"I had a coach at my last job," Chuck replied. "It can be a structured process where you and the coach identify growth areas and work through them, but a coach can also be a sounding board to help you think through different ways of approaching your challenges. It's important to find a good fit, so feel free to talk to Alicia, but you may also want to interview some others until you find someone you like."

Thanking Chuck for the suggestion, Julie headed back to the kitchen for one more cup of coffee before she wrapped up for the day.

That evening as she sat with her journal looking back over the last few weeks, she found herself thinking about an old story her grandfather—a U.S. Marine who had fought in the trenches in the Pacific theater in World War II—had told her many years ago about leadership.

On the beaches of Guadalcanal with the bullets ripping overhead, two marines crouched in a ditch.

"We're getting slaughtered!" shouted the sergeant.

His commanding officer pointed across the field at a nest of machine guns. "You need to take your team across the field and take out those positions!" he yelled back.

The sergeant looked out at the wide swath of open space. He would be totally exposed and his team would be taking a tremendous risk. It was unthinkable. He swallowed hard and turned to his commander. "No one will follow me out there," he said.

His leader looked him in the eyes and said, "Then you go alone and don't look behind you. When you get there, if you find that even one or two of your people have come with you, then you work with them."

Of course Julie knew her job didn't ask her to face down machine guns, but she realized that part of being a leader included having the courage to do hard things, to stick up for her team and for her decisions.

It was a lesson she had heard many times before, but doing it in practice was definitely tougher than doing it in theory.

THE FIFTH TRUTH

The setting sun washed in through the floor-to-ceiling windows, momentarily blinding Julie as she stepped into the gym. She looked around for Chuck and, spotting him over by the front desk, she hitched her backpack up on her shoulder and headed over to meet him. For the last three weeks, things on the team had been running pretty smoothly. Sudha, the new team member, was already taking on some key tasks for the team, and Jamal and Bryce had both stepped up to help teach her the team culture and values. Julie had also spent two incredibly productive meetings working with Maria and Antonella to close some of the gaps between what customers were asking for and what the product could actually currently do. They had made some solid progress on prioritizing the road map, and it was feeling much more like a collaboration these days.

Sure, there were bumps in the road, but Julie could see how things had changed for the better, so she had been looking forward to her monthly update meeting with Chuck. She had been surprised (and honestly a little apprehensive) when he suggested that they take their meeting off-site.

"I know you've had a chance to learn from some great people over the last few months, and I want to show you something I learned that helped me become a better leader," his email had said. "Let's meet up at the rock climbing gym on Central Street after work, and I think you'll be interested in what you can learn there."

Intrigued, Julie had agreed, so here she stood with her gym clothes in her bag, ready to try something new. Chuck introduced her to Jessica, a slim woman in her 20s with a wide smile, sporting a climbing harness and a knit headband. After Julie changed into her gym clothes, Jessica fitted her out with a harness of her own, a pair of climbing shoes, and a belay tool. Julie listened closely as Jessica and Chuck explained how to attach her harness to the climbing rope, and then described the process for belaying.

"The thing about rock climbing," explained Jessica, "is that it's a team effort. There's the climber who's trying to get up the wall, and then there's the person on belay—the one holding the other end of the rope so that you don't come plummeting back down suddenly when you meant to be going up."

Chuck chimed in, "I've been climbing for a few months now, so I'm definitely still a beginner. But it's a surprisingly interesting process. Every time I climb, I learn something about myself, and I see clear parallels to what we do at work. You'll see once you get up on the wall."

After the safety training was complete, Julie felt like she was ready to give it a try. Jessica explained the numbering system that indicated how hard each climb was, so Julie could start with the easier routes, and then move up to tougher ones once she got more comfortable.

Starting up the first route, Julie felt pretty confident. The hand-holds were big and comfortable to grip, and as she climbed up each section, she saw that Chuck was steadily taking up on the safety rope. About halfway up, Julie looked back down and realized that she was more than 20 feet in the air, with another 20 feet still to go. Realizing that a fall from here would be more than just painful, she felt her mouth go dry and her palms start to sweat. Seeing her pause, Chuck called up to her.

"Look up!"

Julie did, realizing that the climb hadn't gotten any harder, she had just gotten anxious knowing she could fall. She focused on the next handhold, keeping her eyes on the top. Slowly and steadily, moving from hold to hold, Julie continued climbing.

When she finally touched the top hold, she slapped the top of the wall.

"I'm up!" she said. It felt great, and she took a moment to savor the accomplishment, looking down at Chuck and giving him a big grin.

"Good job," said Chuck. "Now let go."

Julie was startled. "No way," she said, starting to climb down.

"Really," called Jessica. "It's the best way to come down, and it's good for you to feel the safety ropes doing their job."

Julie hung back slowly, allowing her weight to rest in the harness, and letting go of the handholds. She was no longer holding the wall, and she found that the harness and the top rope held her easily.

"Ready to come down?" asked Chuck.

Julie gave the thumbs up and felt the rope pay out as she dropped back down. She could tell that Chuck was completely in control of the speed, and he was careful not to drop her too quickly. As her feet touched the mat, she felt a huge smile light up her face.

"That was great, can I do another one?"

Julie and Chuck spent the next two hours alternating who was climbing and who was belaying. Julie learned how to be sure that the slack was taken up quickly so Chuck wouldn't have far to fall if he slipped. She also discovered that when she slipped during a tougher climb, she only fell a few inches.

Jessica explained how the mechanics of the top rope system worked, and that it was possible to belay someone even if they weighed much more than you. By then the sun had set, and Julie's hands and arms were tired. She and Chuck wrapped up their last climb, and then headed to the locker rooms to shower and change.

Afterward they sat in the café and, over sandwiches, Chuck told Julie some of the things he had learned from climbing that carried over to work.

Chuck's Story

I started climbing because my son wanted to try it. Unlike swimming or soccer, rock climbing wasn't something I could just drop him off to do. I realized that if he wanted to do it, I was going to need to participate too. The first thing I discovered is that it's all about trust.

Without trust you spend more time looking down than up. My son is 13 and weighs about 50 pounds less than I do. Because of the way the rope system and belay tools work, he can easily hold me up when I come off the wall. But, my first few climbs I wasn't sure. He's a great kid, but how could I be sure he was paying attention when he learned what he was supposed to do? Did he really understand the technique? If I fell unexpectedly was I going to come crashing down on the mat, or would he catch me? I spent a lot of time on those first few climbs focusing down instead of up. But it soon became clear that I could totally count on him— he was right there anytime I lost my grip. By being able to trust that I wouldn't fall, I was suddenly able to get up walls I thought I couldn't do. I had the confidence to try to reach that next hold or hang my full weight on one finger, even when I was 30 feet off the mat.

The same is true with your team. If you don't trust that they are on the same page, doing the right things, and holding the rope for you, you'll spend more time worrying about what's not happening instead of focusing on what moves you up toward your goal. Looking up and forward at your goal is the key, but if you can't trust your team, and they can't trust you, then you start to see all the ways things could go wrong instead of seeing what could go right. You start looking down too much.

Strength is good, but technique is better. The easy climbs are like ladders. They are a series of nice holds, you go up step by step, and before you know it, you're at the top. But once you go up a level or two, strength alone won't take you to the top. Each climb has spots that require you to think, use your whole body, and work your angles to get in position to move up. Sure, if you had all the strength in the world you could pull yourself up by your fingernails, but the harder the climb, the more your brain becomes your most important asset, not your muscles.

We have a mentality in the business world today about working hard and being busy. It's practically a cult. If you're not working 60-70 hours a week, you're not really trying. But more is not better. More hours don't lead to smart work. It most often takes you to burnout, mistakes, and bad decisions.

I have a moment in almost every climb where I'm pretty sure I can't make it. I can see the next hold, but it's too far, too small, or it requires me to leave this nice safe place I just got to. I get this feeling in my stomach that I can't do it—I'm not strong enough, I'm out of breath, I might slip. I look down instead of up. Because it happens in every climb, I've realized that feeling is a lie. I can get past that spot, and when I do, I get to where I want to be. I could quit (and sometimes I do), but I know this is a temporary challenge and if I get over it, the road to the top is clear.

Every company, and sometimes every project, has that moment. That sticky bit when it all starts to go off the rails. Getting through the tough bit takes grit. It's the people who don't stop when it gets hard who are still standing at the top.

Plan, try, fail; adapt, try again, succeed. When I first started climbing more advanced routes, I would just launch up them like

I had with the beginner climbs. I would get halfway up and find myself in an awkward spot with no clear path forward. In bouldering (lower climbs where you don't need a harness and a rope), each route is called a "problem" and it's typical to see people lying on the mats resting between attempts, gazing up at the route and mentally working through it.

Look first and plan what you think will work. It probably won't work the first time, but then you can adapt and try again. Sometimes it takes a couple of tries, sometimes many, but you'll get there eventually.

There is no competition. I was once two-thirds of the way up a route that I had never finished when I realized a woman at the bottom was watching me climb. I was stuck at a spot and trying some different grips to try and reach for a hold that was just a few inches too far. I got my fingers on it but couldn't hold on, so I came off the wall and came back down. When I got to the bottom she said to me, "I got stuck there too, and I wanted to see what you were going to try."

It's a common conversation—a mutual acceptance that we are all trying to figure each challenge out every time we go up. I feel great when I get to the top of a climb, but I never feel like I'm competing with anyone. Sure, there are people who are better climbers, who have better technique, who are stronger, but they just climb different routes than I do.

This concept is a little less true in business. There is competition, at least at a basic level. While everyone loves a wide-open market, if no one is doing what you're doing, it's more likely than not that you are on the wrong track. But with that said, unless you are actively going after the same client at the same moment, there is huge value in the community of practice concept. Finding people who are working in your space gives you the opportunity to learn new ideas, and to gain insights. No one succeeds working completely alone.

Julie and Chuck finished up their dinner and walked back to the train station together. Chuck hopped on the northbound train, while Julie sat on a bench waiting for her train to arrive. She felt tired but satisfied. She thought she finally understood one of the most important lessons about leadership—trust and mistakes are both necessary. You can't take risks if you don't trust your team, and if you don't take those risks, you don't learn from them. Not everything you try is going to be successful, but you've got to have trust to try anything at all.

Back in her home office, Julie wrote one more line in her journal.

THE TRUTH ABOUT MANAGEMENT

Vision: Define the values your team shares and measure everything you do against those values.

Team: Know your team members' strengths and focus on clearing the obstacles to their success.

Goals: Focus on the outputs and recognize each successful achievement.

Learn and Adapt: Develop the habit of learning from each day's work and focus on growth, not perfection.

Trust: Without trust, there is no team.

Sitting back in her chair, Julie laid the pen down on her desk and flipped through her journal. Looking back to last year, before her promotion, she could see the evolution of her perspective, from confident to overwhelmed, to determined, and now optimistic. It had been a challenging time, but she had to smile. It certainly hadn't been easy, but learning these truths had definitely been worth the effort.

THE TRUTH ABOUT MANAGEMENT

Julie stepped into the crowded coffee shop, pausing for a moment to remove her coat and take a deep breath of the warm, aromatic air. Stepping up to the counter, she ordered coffee, hesitated for a moment, and then added a cheese Danish as well, all while keeping her eye out for Sarah. It had taken a few weeks to find time on both their calendars, and Julie was excited to share some news on her progress at work.

Spotting a couple just leaving a table in the corner, Julie headed over, waving at Sarah as she came through the door. Settling down with her breakfast, Julie waited for her former boss to make it through the line.

"Not fired after all?" quipped Sarah as she sat down, smiling.

Julie smiled back. "Nope. I think I'm starting to get the hang of this management thing."

Sarah nodded. "It's tougher than it looks, but it sounds like you've learned some things. I'd love to hear about it."

"When I saw you on the train back in September, I was in way over my head," Julie began. "I thought all I had to do was work harder and stay on top of all the tasks my team was responsible for. I wasn't thinking about leading a team, I was thinking about keeping track of a lot of tasks. I had become a master juggler, and I thought I was doing a great job because I was keeping track of everything. But when Susan quit I realized that it isn't just about getting all the tasks done."

Sarah nodded her agreement. "It's easy to get sucked into feeling productive because you're so busy. But just because you're busy, it doesn't mean you're doing the right things."

"Exactly," said Julie. "After I met your team, I realized that mine didn't have that same sense of shared purpose. We hadn't been thinking about the values that we had in common, or how our work contributed to the goals of the whole company. We were just each working in our own little bubble. Having a clear understanding of that purpose and vision helped me figure out where we should be focusing our time."

Julie paused to take a sip of her coffee.

"Meeting Mike was also an eye opener for me. I've always felt like I have to be smarter—or at least more knowledgeable—than everyone else on my team or else they'll wonder why I'm the leader instead of them. But seeing how Mike operates, how he values the expertise of everyone on his team, and how they respect his role in seeing the big picture, I realized I was wrong. I don't have to pretend I know everything."

"That was a big one for me, too," Sarah said. "I always felt like such a fraud in my first management job. I wanted to be the one with all the answers. When I realized I didn't have to know it all, it was a big relief!

"I also think some people push themselves to become managers because that's how they can make more money, or show that they are making progress in their careers," Sarah continued. "So they get into management because they think they have to, not because they enjoy it."

Nodding, Julie went on. "Mike introduced me to his sister-in-law, Carolina, who had such an interesting perspective on managing to results. I knew goals were important before I took on this job, but talking to Carolina really brought home to me how important it is to not just have goals, but to align them with the vision, and with the needs of the people on the team. I think working virtually makes it even more important to communicate in a clear way, but it also made me think differently about how our team communicates and operates. It's easy to think that just because we are in the same office space, we are communicating regularly. But it's not whether we talk every day, it's what we talk about, and how we hold ourselves accountable that matters."

"Accountability is a tough one," agreed Sarah. "Especially when you are managing people who used to be your peers. If you don't set clear expectations, you can't be consistent in how you respond."

"The last few weeks I've had my eyes opened to all kinds of aspects of management that I never considered," Julie said. "I learned one of the most interesting truths about management at a football game!"

Sarah laughed. "Once you start really paying attention to leadership, you see examples of it everywhere, both good and bad."

Julie shared her conversation with Marcus, and how he approached coaching football.

"It makes complete sense when you think about it," said Julie. "It's a constant process of preparing, then doing work—in their case, running plays, in our case, managing projects—and finally looking at what you did and seeing how you can do it better. It made me realize that we don't spend enough time on the third part—the review and learning process often falls off the plate when we're busy trying to move on to the next thing."

They both got up to refill their coffee. When they got back to the table, Sarah brought up the topic that had been the catalyst for her pursuit of the truth about management in the first place.

"What happened with Susan?"

Julie sighed. "She took the new position. HR offered her more money and tried to convince her to stay, but she really felt like she needed a change. I can't blame her; looking back on the last six months after everything I've learned, I know I was doing a lot of things that were frustrating to her. I also think she believed she could have taken on my job and done it better than I have."

"What about Chuck?" asked Sarah. "Does he agree that things are on a better track now?"

"It's funny you should ask," said Julie. "He and I went rock climbing earlier this month, and we talked a lot about trust. I know it's not the last lesson I'll learn about being a manager, but I really felt like it brought things full circle. You can do all of the other things you're supposed to do, but if you don't trust your team members, or they don't trust you, nothing really works."

"That's absolutely true," said Sarah. "It takes time to build trust on a team. Time for people to see that you're reliable when you commit to something, and that you're consistent and fair when you evaluate their work."

"It's a disciplined process of caring about people," said Julie thoughtfully. "One of the things Chuck said to me earlier on in the process was that he put me in this role because he believes I care about the work and about the people. At the time, I didn't really see how that was going to help me be a good manager, but the more I think about it, the more important it seems."

Sarah smiled. "That's a nice way of putting it. People always know when you don't care. If you've checked out and are just going through the motions, you can expect that the people on your team will do the same. But if you genuinely care about them, about their success, and about the success of the organization, you can't really go wrong."

The two women stood, and Julie gave Sarah a warm hug.

"I'm so glad you were on the train that day. I can't thank you enough."

Sarah gave her a warm smile. "Managers make all the difference in how people feel about work. People don't usually quit because the company is bad; they quit because they are frustrated with the person who has the most influence on their day-to-day job. There's a lot more to learn, but I know you're on the right track."

EPILOGUE
NOT ANOTHER RAINY DAY

The bright early-summer sun warmed Julie's shoulders as she walked through the public gardens. She had a bounce in her step that was partly the weather, partly a result of the meeting she had that morning with Chuck.

"I'd like to say I told you so," he had quipped, handing her the letter offering her a raise. "But I don't want to take away anything from you. You've worked hard over the last six months and it shows. I've been truly impressed, both with how your team has performed, and how you're stepping up into a leadership role within the organization. How does it feel?"

Julie smiled, thinking about that day on the train nearly a year ago, when she had believed that at best she was going to be demoted, and at worst, fired for her performance. While she knew she wasn't perfect, Julie also knew that she had come a long way.

Sudha, the newest member of the team, was rapidly coming up to speed. Both Bryce and Jamal had lived up to their commitments to step up in Susan's absence and become mentors to Sudha as she learned the team culture and the values they shared.

Julie was also proud of how things had improved with the sales team. Their weekly meetings and regular project debriefs had created a spirit of collaboration between the two teams. Gone were the days when a sales rep would hand her a project plan full of unrealistic deliverables and impossible deadlines. Instead, Julie was part of the conversation from the beginning, which made the scoping process far more accurate.

It hadn't been all sunshine and roses. While she had learned a lot about how to approach her role, and continued to learn from her coach, as well as training programs and webinars, Julie knew she still made mistakes, and that there was much more to learn. But by letting go of trying to be perfect, and by focusing on that disciplined process of caring about people, she felt like both she and her team were more resilient—more able to deal with the inevitable bad days and bumps in the road.

As she made her way across the park, the coffee kiosk came into sight and she saw the familiar face she was looking for. Susan had emailed her earlier in the week, asking to meet. She hadn't said why, but Julie had an idea of what it was she wanted to discuss.

Giving her friend and former colleague a quick hug, Julie went up to the counter to order a cup of coffee. Stirring in cream and sugar, she returned to the table where Susan was sitting.

"How are things going?" Julie asked. "I want to hear all about the new job!"

Susan smiled wryly. "I'll tell you all about it, but I want to start out by saying I'm sorry for giving you such a hard time last year."

Julie laughed. "Actually, if it wasn't for you and your decision to quit, I'm not sure I would be in the position I'm in now. I didn't realize it at the time, but that was probably the best thing that could have happened."

Susan nodded. "I heard things are going really well for you. I met Bryce for drinks after work the other day, and he said he's really happy with how things are on the team these days." She paused. "He was the one who suggested I reach out to you."

Julie raised an eyebrow. "Are things not going so well in the new job?"

Susan blew out a sigh. "No they aren't. I had no idea it was so hard to lead a team. I really envied you when Chuck tapped you to take over the team at Midora. I thought you had the opportunity of a lifetime, and if I'm honest, I thought he should have chosen me instead. When I was working for you, I was constantly frustrated because I thought I could do it better. Last month, when they asked me to lead my team at my new company, I was thrilled. But now that I'm in the job, I feel like I've lost all my confidence. I used to know exactly what to do every day. Now I feel like I'm in the dark."

Julie nodded with sympathy. "I know that feeling."

Susan shook her head. "I know I'm not getting it right, but I just don't know how or why. It's so frustrating. I've read some books, I took a class in time management, but I just don't feel like I can even put my finger on what I'm missing."

She looked at Julie. "I was complaining about all of this the other night, and Bryce said I should talk to you. He said that you had made some big changes in the last few months with your approach, and that it seems to be working. I have to ask, what did you do?"

Julie paused, on the verge of starting to try to tell Susan the stories of the people who had told her the truth about management. She knew that what she had heard was a big part of how and why she had changed her mindset and approach to managing. But she knew it wouldn't have the same impact if Susan heard those stories secondhand. And, she also knew that meeting the same people might not help Susan the way it had helped her. So instead, she asked a question:

"Who was the best manager you ever worked for? You don't have to answer now, but start there. Reach out to that person and ask if you can meet to talk. I thought I knew the truth about management when I took that team lead role. I thought I was ready, and that it wasn't going to be that hard. But being successful as a leader isn't just about time management or delegating tasks or keeping track of projects. It's about seeing things from a different perspective."

Susan nodded. "That makes sense. And would you be willing to tell me what you've learned too?"

Julie smiled. "Of course! As long as you know that I'm still learning myself, and I know I will be for a long time."

KATY'S FAVORITE MANAGEMENT BOOKS

Drive: The Surprising Truth About What Motivates Us
by Daniel Pink

I bought this book after watching Dan Pink's amazing TED Talk on what science knows and business doesn't. I have a degree in psychology, and I often feel like the ability to understand how people think, what motivates them, and what frustrates them is the most important skill for a manager. The thing I love about this book is that the author draws you in with great stories.

The Five Dysfunctions of a Team: A Leadership Fable
by Patrick Lencioni

I was assigned this book as part of an executive development program I was lucky enough to be a part of. At the time, I was working for a start-up organization and the whole management team was under 30 years old. It was a room full of smart, passionate, driven people, but we hadn't figured out how to pull in the same direction. Even though we all had great respect for one another, our daily interactions were stressful. Our executive coach gave us this book, and I still remember the feeling I had as I read it—it just seemed to explain exactly why we were all so frustrated. Pat did a terrific job of blending a great story with a solid framework. It's one of the best books about team dynamics I have ever read.

The One Minute Manager
by Ken Blanchard and Spencer Johnson

My dad gave me this book when I was in college while I was managing the sailing program I wrote about in this book's introduction. It is such a simple concept, and even though it's now decades old, the basic idea in the book is still useful and relevant. Large organizations have recently started trending away from annual performance reviews in favor of encouraging more frequent conversations between managers and their team members. Focusing on small adjustments, giving regular feedback, and connecting in conversation is the key to individual development, so I was glad to see the updated edition in 2015.

The Reality Based Rules of the Workforce:
Know What Boosts Your Value, Kills Your Chances,
and Will Make You Happier
by Cy Wakeman

I was sent Cy Wakeman's book to review while I was doing a series of book reviews on my blog. It is not for the faint of heart—Cy pulls no punches on personal accountability. What I love about the book is that it delivers such a strong message about how your happiness at work is in your hands. It's easy to read articles about low engagement, and to believe somehow that work is just supposed to be frustrating, or that it's all the fault of HR or senior leadership if we don't feel engaged. But Cy's message—that we are each responsible for how we feel about our work and we have the power to change our own attitudes—is both refreshing and empowering.

The Art of Racing in the Rain
by Garth Stein

The Art of Racing in the Rain isn't actually a management book. It's the story of a very wise dog, and his sometimes not so wise human. But there are some amazing ideas in this book that are applicable to management in a fundamental way. I have the quote "The car goes where the eyes go" over my desk. Our careers and our lives go where our focus goes, and that is the essence of leadership. There's also a great story about zebras, but I can't explain that one in just a paragraph—you'll have to read it for yourself.

Start With Why: How Great Leaders Inspire Everyone to Take Action
by Simon Sinek

We've all felt that moment when we see a product and just want to have it. Simon Sinek uses Apple's marketing as an example to help us understand a fundamental truth about how our brains work. Similar to Daniel Pink's book, *Start With Why* gets to the root of why we want to do things, which in turn helps us realize what we need to do if we want to influence others.

The 7 Habits of Highly Effective People: Powerful Lessons in Personal Change
by Stephen Covey

This book appears on almost every list of management books, and for good reason. From the fable of the rocks in the jar to the concept of circles of influence, these ideas are not so much about management as they are about getting things accomplished. They create a solid foundation for anyone who aspires to a leadership role.

ABOUT THE AUTHOR

Katy Tynan is an author, speaker, consultant, and coach, as well as an internationally recognized expert on how work is evolving. In a world where 70 percent of employees are disengaged, Katy helps organizations ditch out-of-date management practices and create an inspiring, engaging culture.

Over her 20-year career in IT and operations consulting, Katy has advised hundreds of organizations on how to find innovative solutions leveraging technology and human capital for competitive advantage. She has been part of multiple successful start-up exits, including Winphoria Networks (acquired by Motorola in 2003) and Thrive Networks (acquired by Staples in 2007).

Katy is currently the managing director of CoreAxis Consulting, a leading talent strategy consulting firm based in Southborough, Massachusetts. She is the author of *Survive Your Promotion! The 90 Day Success Plan for New Managers* and *How Did I Not See This Coming? A New Manager's Guide to Avoiding Total Disaster*.

31901064529987